I0008261

Cybersecurity

Bible

A Comprehensive Guide to Safeguarding Your Digital
World from Antivirus to Zero-Day Attacks

Blaze Hawthorn

Copyright © 2024 **Blaze Hawthorn**

All Rights Reserved

This book or parts thereof may not be reproduced in any form, stored in any retrieval system, or transmitted in any form by any means—electronic, mechanical, photocopy, recording, or otherwise—without prior written permission of the publisher, except as provided by United States of America copyright law and fair use.

Disclaimer and Terms of Use

The author and publisher of this book and the accompanying materials have used their best efforts in preparing this book. The author and publisher make no representation or warranties with respect to the accuracy, applicability, fitness, or completeness of the contents of this book. The information contained in this book is strictly for informational purposes. Therefore, if you wish to apply the ideas contained in this book, you are taking full responsibility for your actions.

Printed in the United States of America

TABLE OF CONTENTS

INTRODUCTION

Amidst the era of widespread technological integration into various facets of our daily existence, ranging from interpersonal communication to vital infrastructure, the significance of cybersecurity cannot be emphasized enough. The advent of the digital revolution has ushered in an era of unprecedented convenience and connectivity. However, it has also given rise to novel vulnerabilities and threats that were previously unknown. Cybersecurity, consequently, serves as the primary defense against malevolent individuals who aim to exploit these vulnerabilities for personal benefit. Cybersecurity encompasses a comprehensive array of practices, technologies, and processes that are meticulously devised to safeguard networks, systems, data, and individuals from any form of unauthorized access, malicious attacks, and potential harm. The approach encompasses a comprehensive range of strategies that integrate technical solutions, including firewalls and encryption, with a strong emphasis on human vigilance and adherence to organizational policies.

The importance of cybersecurity extends well beyond individual or organizational considerations; it is essential for protecting national security, ensuring economic stability, and promoting societal well-being. With the increasing dependence on digital technologies, the potential consequences of cyber threats are also expanding. Cyber-attacks can result in significant consequences, ranging from the disruption of essential services to the theft of sensitive information or the perpetration of large-scale fraud. The ever-changing cyber threat landscape is a result of technological advancements, the widespread use of interconnected devices, and the increasing sophistication of malicious actors. Conventional security risks like viruses, worms, and malware continue to exist, but they have been accompanied by emerging, more deceptive variations of cybercrime, such as ransomware, phishing, and social engineering attacks. In addition, the advent of the Internet of Things (IoT) has brought forth a multitude of security challenges. With billions of devices, ranging from smart appliances to industrial control systems, now susceptible to exploitation, the need for robust security measures has become paramount. The field of cybersecurity encounters a multitude of challenges and vulnerabilities, which arise from a combination of technical and human factors. Various factors such as vulnerabilities in software and hardware, inadequate security protocols, and a lack of user awareness collectively contribute to the overall risk landscape. In addition, the growing interconnectedness of systems necessitates that a breach in one domain can potentially result in a ripple effect that impacts entire networks or industries.

Implementing Effective Cybersecurity Measures

To effectively address the ever-evolving landscape of cyber threats, it is imperative to adopt a proactive and multi-layered approach to cybersecurity. The following items are included:

1. Firstly, Risk assessment is a crucial step in developing effective security measures for an organization or system. It involves gaining a comprehensive understanding of the specific risks and vulnerabilities that may be present. By identifying and analyzing these factors, organizations can then implement targeted security measures to mitigate potential threats.

2. Establishing comprehensive security policies and procedures is crucial for ensuring effective data protection, access control, incident response, and employee training. By implementing clear guidelines, organizations can establish a strong foundation for maintaining a robust security posture.

3. Technical controls involve the implementation of various technological solutions to enhance the security posture and protect against cyber threats. These solutions encompass the deployment of firewalls, antivirus software, encryption mechanisms, and intrusion detection systems. By incorporating these technical measures, organizations can bolster their defenses and mitigate potential risks.

4. The implementation of ongoing monitoring of network traffic and system activity facilitates the prompt identification of any suspicious behavior or potential security breaches, thereby enabling timely intervention.

5. The implementation of a well-defined incident response plan is crucial to promptly and efficiently address security incidents. This proactive approach helps to mitigate potential damage and streamline the recovery process.

6. In light of the interconnectedness of the digital ecosystem, organizations, government agencies, and cybersecurity professionals must engage in collaborative efforts to share threat intelligence and exchange best practices.

7. The implementation of comprehensive user education initiatives that focus on familiarizing individuals with prevalent cyber threats, promoting secure browsing practices, and emphasizing the significance of robust passwords can effectively minimize the impact of human error in cybersecurity breaches.

CHAPTER ONE
GETTING STARTED WITH CYBERSECURITY

Overview

Chapter one discusses what cybersecurity is all about including why it is important for your day-to-day life, the fundamentals of cybersecurity, terms and terminologies, and so much more.

What Is Cybersecurity?

Cybersecurity is a critical concern for all stakeholders, ranging from governments and large corporations to small business owners, employees, and even individuals in their homes.

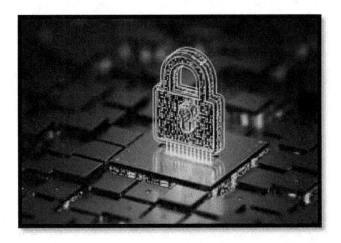

We reside in a world characterized by unparalleled interconnectedness. Each year, we observe an increasing number of everyday devices being connected to the Internet. Simultaneously, nearly every aspect of our lives is electronically tracked. This encompasses all of our health records, financial information, power consumption data, clothing choices, arrival times at home, travel destinations, and other relevant details. With the proper data, machines can construct profiles that possess a deeper understanding of individuals than we have of ourselves. This underscores the significance of individual knowledge and action. Your data is spread across more locations than ever, and it is your responsibility to ensure its protection. It is important to take responsibility for being aware of the platforms where you share your data, comprehending the potential consequences of such sharing, and taking all possible measures to mitigate the associated risks for yourself. For companies, cyberattacks are becoming increasingly common and costly. Gartner reports that enterprises are projected to allocate over $1.7 billion globally towards cybersecurity in 2020, representing a growth of 10.7% compared to the previous year. There is a rapidly increasing number of unmanaged and unprotected IoT (Internet of Things) devices being used within companies, thus resulting in a significantly expanding attack landscape. Cybercriminals and nation-states are increasingly focusing their efforts on targeting Internet of Things (IoT) devices, primarily due to the inherent lack of security measures implemented in these devices. I have observed instances where vending machines have been used for data exfiltration. According to our findings, there has been a significant increase of 300% in IoT attacks during the initial period of 2018. Due to the potential of cyberattacks to severely impact businesses, organizations are increasingly acknowledging the importance of prioritizing cybersecurity training and recruitment. In recent years, the field of security has undergone a significant transformation, evolving from a technical discipline within the world of information technology to a crucial component of business risk management. It is justified to be concerned, as approximately five million data records are lost or stolen worldwide daily. At a larger scale, even politics, diplomacy, and social cohesion are at stake. We observe nations engaging in the unauthorized acquisition of undisclosed quantities of confidential information and intellectual property from one another, exerting influence over each other's electoral processes, and even impacting our wider social discourse. Machines can be utilized on a large scale to impact nearly every aspect of our society, extending even to the level of individual individuals. This situation highlights the importance of addressing security risks.

Working in the field of cybersecurity

Now, let us shift our focus to the field of cybersecurity careers, beginning with the reasons why it is a profession that embraces individuals from diverse backgrounds, including those without technical expertise. Next, we will discuss the job outlook and specialties that you can explore.

The Value of Transitioning from a Non-Technical Background

It is erroneous to consider security as a singular career path. There are numerous distinct career paths within the field of security, providing opportunities for individuals who have a strong interest in safeguarding our cyber infrastructure. The demand for security professionals is rapidly increasing and shows no signs of slowing down, indicating a promising future for individuals pursuing careers in this field.

If you believe that possessing a computer science degree and a decade of technical experience is a prerequisite for contemplating a career in this field, we implore you to reconsider your stance. Implementing effective security measures on a large scale necessitates a combination of expertise in law, psychology, sociology, technology, and organizational sciences. Cybersecurity presents a diverse range of opportunities for individuals with both technical and non-technical backgrounds. Many individuals tend to focus on technical operators and incident response engineers as the primary career paths in cybersecurity. However, it is important to note that the field also requires program managers, software developers, professional communicators, data scientists, systems analysts, and more. Furthermore, it is important to note that there are additional career opportunities within a security company, such as product management, marketing, public relations, and sales. Having a non-technical background can be advantageous as it allows you to bring unique perspectives and abilities to the table, setting you apart from others. The security team comprises individuals with diverse backgrounds, including librarians, journalists, lawyers, and control systems experts. We hire them because we require those skill sets in the security career fields. For example, security practitioners can cover policy and law, while others can build large-scale distributed systems, find security flaws, or focus on finding evil that's lurking where it doesn't belong.

Cybersecurity Fundamentals

Network and Security Concepts

Information Assurance Fundamentals

Authentication, authorization, and non-repudiation are tools that system designers can use to uphold system security concerning confidentiality, integrity, and availability. Understanding each of these six concepts and how they relate to one another helps security professionals design and implement secure systems. Each component is crucial to the overall security, as the failure of any one component can potentially compromise the entire system. It is imperative for individuals responsible for safeguarding an information system to possess a comprehensive understanding of three fundamental concepts, commonly referred to as the CIA triad: confidentiality, integrity, and availability. Information security professionals are committed to ensuring the protection of these principles for each system they safeguard. Furthermore, security professionals must have a comprehensive understanding of three fundamental concepts to effectively implement the CIA principles: authentication, authorization, and non-repudiation. Within this section, we will elucidate each of these concepts and expound upon their interrelationships within the realm of digital security. All definitions used here originate from the National Information Assurance Glossary (NIAG) published by the United States. Committee on National Security Systems.

Authentication is a crucial aspect of any secure system, as it plays a key role in verifying the source of a message or confirming the identity of an individual. The National Institute of Authentication and Governance (NIAG) defines authentication as a security measure that is designed to establish the validity of a transmission, message, or originator. It is also a means of verifying an individual's authorization to receive specific categories of information. Numerous methods can be utilized to authenticate an individual. In each method, the authenticator issues a challenge that an individual must respond to. This challenge typically involves requesting a piece of information that can only be provided by authenticated users. These pieces of information typically fall into the three classifications known as factors of authentication. When an authentication system requires more than one of these factors, the security community classifies it as a system requiring multi factor authentication. Two instances of the same factor, such as a password combined with a user's mother's maiden name, are not considered multi-factor authentication. However, combining a fingerprint scan and a personal identification number (PIN) is considered multi factor authentication as it validates both something the user is (the owner of that fingerprint) and something the user knows (a PIN). Authentication also applies to the process of verifying the origin or source of a message, such as a network packet or email. At a low level, message authentication systems cannot rely on the same factors that apply to human authentication. Message authentication systems often rely on cryptographic signatures, which consist of a digest or hash of the message generated with a secret key. Given that only one individual possesses the key responsible for generating the signature, the recipient is capable of verifying the identity of the sender of a message.

Without a robust authentication system, it is not possible to establish trust in the identity of a user or the origin of a message.

- **Authorization**: Authentication pertains to the process of verifying identities, whereas authorization focuses on determining the specific permissions granted to a user. The National Institute of Accountants and Auditors (NIAG) define authorization as "**access privileges granted to a user, program, or process**." Once a secure system successfully authenticates users, it must also determine the privileges they possess. For example, an online banking application will authenticate a user based on their credentials, but it must then determine the accounts to which that user has access. In addition, the system determines the actions that the user can take concerning those accounts, such as viewing balances and making transfers.

- **Nonrepudiation**: Consider a scenario in which Alice is purchasing a car from Bob and signs a contract stipulating that she will pay $20,000 for the car and assume ownership on Thursday. If Alice later decides not to purchase the vehicle, she may assert that her signature has been forged and that she bears no responsibility for the contractual agreement. To counter her assertion, Bob could provide evidence that a notary public verified Alice's identity and affixed their official stamp on the document as an indication of this verification. In this case, the notary's stamp has bestowed upon the contract the property of nonrepudiation, which is defined by the NIAG as "**the assurance that the sender of data is provided with proof of delivery and the recipient is provided with proof of the sender's identity so that neither can later deny having processed the data**." In digital communications, it is not feasible for a notary to physically stamp each transmitted message. However, the concept of non-repudiation remains crucial and indispensable. To fulfill this requirement, secure systems typically rely on asymmetric (or public key) cryptography. While symmetric key systems use a single key to encrypt and decrypt data, asymmetric systems use a key pair. These systems use one key (private) to sign data and employ the other key (public) for the verification of data. If the same key can both sign and verify the content of a message, the sender can assert that anyone who has access to the key could easily have forged it. Asymmetric key systems possess the property of nonrepudiation because the signer of a message can maintain the confidentiality of their private key.

- **Confidentiality** is a widely recognized concept, known to many individuals, even those outside of the security industry. The National Institute of Aging (NIAG) defines confidentiality as "the assurance that information is not disclosed to unauthorized individuals, processes, or devices."

Ensuring that unauthorized parties do not have access to a piece of information is a complex task. It is easiest to comprehend when dissected into three major steps. Firstly, the information must possess robust protections that are capable of preventing certain users from accessing it. Secondly, it is imperative to establish limitations to restrict access to the information solely to individuals who possess the necessary authorization to view it. Third, it is imperative to establish an authentication system to effectively verify the identity of individuals who have been granted access to the data. Authentication and authorization, as previously described in this section, are crucial for maintaining confidentiality. However, the concept of confidentiality primarily focuses on concealing or protecting the information. One way to protect information is by storing it in a private location or on a private network that is limited to those who have legitimate access to the information. If an organization needs to transmit data over a public network, it is advisable to utilize a key known only to authorize parties for encrypting the data. When it comes to transmitting information over the Internet, ensuring its security can be achieved through various means. One such method is the utilization of a virtual private network (VPN), which encrypts all data exchanged between endpoints. Another option is to employ encrypted email systems, which restrict access to messages solely to their intended recipients. If confidential information is being physically transported outside of its protected location, such as when employees transfer backup tapes between facilities, organizations should encrypt the data to ensure that it remains secure if it falls into the hands of unauthorized users.

The preservation of confidentiality in digital information necessitates the implementation of controls in the physical realm as well. Shoulder surfing, also known as the practice of observing an individual's computer screen by looking over their shoulder, is a non-technical method utilized by attackers to gather sensitive and confidential information. Physical threats, such as theft, also pose a risk to confidentiality. The potential ramifications of a breach of confidentiality are contingent upon the sensitivity of the safeguarded data. A breach in credit card numbers, such as the case of the Heartland Payment Systems processing system in 2008, has the potential to lead to lawsuits with significant financial settlements reaching millions of dollars.

Integrity is a crucial concept in the realm of information security. Specifically, it refers to data integrity, which involves ensuring that stored data remains accurate and free from any unauthorized modifications.

The National Information Assurance Glossary (NIAG) provides the following definition of integrity:

The quality of an Information System (IS) is determined by the logical correctness and reliability of the operating system, the logical completeness of the hardware and software implementing the protection mechanisms, and the consistency of the data structures and occurrence of the stored data. Note that, in a formal security mode, integrity is interpreted more narrowly to mean protection against unauthorized modification or destruction of information. This principle, which relies on authentication, authorization, and nonrepudiation as the keys to maintaining integrity, prevents those without authorization from modifying data. By bypassing an authentication system or escalating privileges beyond those normally granted to them, an attacker can threaten the integrity of data. Software flaws and vulnerabilities can result in unintended data integrity losses and can expose a system to unauthorized modifications. Programs typically tightly control, when a user has read-to-write access to particular data, but software vulnerability might make it possible to circumvent that control. As an illustration, an attacker can exploit a Structured Query Language (SQL) injection vulnerability to extract, alter, or add information to a database. Compromising the integrity of data at rest or in a message in transit can have significant repercussions. If it were possible to modify a funds transfer message passing between a user and his or her online banking website, an attacker could exploit that privilege to their advantage. The attacker can hijack the transfer and steal the transferred funds by altering the account number of the recipient of the funds listed in the message to the attacker's bank account number. Ensuring the integrity of this type of message is crucial to any secure system.

Availability: Information systems must be accessible to users for these systems to provide any value. If a system is experiencing downtime or slow response times, it is unable to deliver the expected level of service. The National Institute of Administration and Governance (NIAG) provides a comprehensive definition of availability as "the provision of timely and reliable access to data and information services for authorized users." Attacks on availability are somewhat different from those on integrity and confidentiality. The most widely recognized form of attack on availability is a denial of service (DoS) attack. A Denial of Service (DoS) attack can manifest in various forms, all of which aim to disrupt a system in a manner that hinders legitimate users from accessing it. One form of Denial of Service (DoS) attack is resource exhaustion, whereby an attacker overwhelms a system to the point that it no longer responds to legitimate requests. The resources in question may include memory, central processing unit (CPU) time, network bandwidth, and/or any other component that an attacker can influence. One example of a Denial of Service (DoS) attack is network flooding. During this type of attack, the attacker sends an excessive amount of network traffic to the targeted system, causing the network to become saturated and preventing legitimate requests from getting through.

Understanding the components of the CIA triad and the underlying concepts of how to protect these principles is crucial for every security professional. Each component functions as a foundational element that supports the overall security of a system. If an attacker successfully breaches any of the pillars, the security of the system will be compromised. Authentication, authorization, and non-repudiation are tools that system designers can utilize to uphold these pillars. It is necessary to have a comprehensive understanding of how all of these concepts interact with each other to effectively utilize them.

The Evolution of Cyber Threats: From Early Days to Modern Warfare

Within the expansive and constantly evolving world of cyberspace, the notion of security has emerged as of utmost importance. With the continuous progress of technology, there is a corresponding evolution in the strategies and incentives of individuals who aim to exploit it for nefarious ends. The evolution of cyber threats is a complex process influenced by various factors, including technological progress, geopolitical dynamics, and the continuous ingenuity of malicious actors. The history of cyber threats spans from the initial emergence of computer viruses to the current use of advanced cyber warfare strategies by nation-states. This chronicle serves as a testament to the perpetual requirement for unwavering vigilance and continuous innovation within the domain of cybersecurity.

The Origins: Viruses and Worms

The origins of cyber threats can be traced back to the nascent stages of computing. During the 1970s and 1980s, the emergence of personal computers marked the introduction of the initial occurrences of malicious software, commonly referred to as malware. One of the earliest documented occurrences was the Creeper virus, which infiltrated ARPANET, the predecessor to the internet, in 1971. The Creeper malware prominently presented the message "I am the Creeper, endeavor to apprehend me if you are able!" on compromised computer systems, signifying the commencement of a novel epoch in the realm of cybersecurity. During the 1980s, the widespread adoption of personal computers resulted in a rise in the occurrence of viruses and worms. The initial iterations of malware were commonly disseminated via compromised floppy disks and were contingent upon human engagement for proliferation. The Morris Worm, which was released in 1988 by Robert Tappan Morris, is widely regarded as one of the most notorious instances of this period. The worm successfully exploited vulnerabilities present in Unix systems, resulting in the infection of a significant number of computers and subsequently causing extensive disruption.

An Analysis of the Escalation of Cybercrime: Strategies for Exploitation and Financial Gain

With the increasing accessibility of the internet in the 1990s, the avenues for cybercriminals also expanded. The advent of e-commerce and online banking has created a conducive environment for exploitation, as malicious actors have actively sought to capitalize on vulnerabilities within online systems. The emergence of phishing attacks, which deceived users into disclosing sensitive information like passwords and credit card numbers, represented a notable change in strategies. During the late 1990s and early 2000s, there was a notable increase in cybercrime, which was primarily fueled by the growing interconnectivity of digital systems. The proliferation of malware, exemplified by notorious cases like the ILOVEYOU worm, as well as the Code Red and Nimda worms, has brought attention to the escalating danger of rapidly spreading malicious software within the realm of the internet. The aforementioned attacks resulted in significant financial losses amounting to billions of dollars, thereby emphasizing the imperative for enhanced cybersecurity protocols.

State-Sponsored Cyber Warfare: A New Frontier

The cyber threat landscape has undergone significant changes in recent years due to the rise of state-sponsored cyber warfare. Nation-states have progressively utilized cyberspace as a strategic tool to accomplish their objectives, encompassing activities such as espionage, sabotage, and even warfare. The Stuxnet worm, which was first identified in 2010, serves as a prime example of the advanced capabilities possessed by cyber weapons sponsored by nation-states. The Stuxnet malware, a collaborative effort between the United States and Israel, was specifically designed to infiltrate and disrupt Iran's nuclear facilities. Its primary objective was to inflict substantial harm on the centrifuges employed for uranium enrichment. The use of cyber weapons by nation-states has resulted in the convergence of conventional warfare and cyber warfare, giving rise to intricate legal and ethical dilemmas. The increasing prevalence of advanced cyber capabilities has also raised concerns regarding the possibility of escalation and unintended repercussions in the event of a cyber-conflict.

The Era of Advanced Persistent Threats: Targeted Attacks and Espionage

In addition to state-sponsored cyber warfare, the emergence of advanced persistent threats (APTs) has significantly added complexity to the cybersecurity environment. Advanced Persistent Threats (APTs) are highly sophisticated and protracted cyber-attacks that are carried out by nation-states or well-financed entities with clearly defined objectives. APT attacks, in contrast to conventional cybercrime, are distinguished by their methodical approach and unwavering determination. Rather than focusing on immediate financial gain, APTs exhibit a patient and persistent nature. Advanced Persistent Threat (APT) groups employ a diverse range of tactics to accomplish their objectives. These tactics encompass targeted phishing campaigns, exploitation of zero-day vulnerabilities, and the utilization of supply chain attacks. The aforementioned attacks are frequently customized to target particular organizations or individuals and possess the ability to evade detection for extended periods, ranging from several months to even several years. The individuals responsible for Advanced Persistent Threats (APTs) encompass a wide spectrum, ranging from nation-states that sponsor these activities intending to acquire valuable and confidential data, to criminal syndicates involved in acts of industrial espionage.

The Future of Cyber Threats: Challenges and Opportunities

With the continuous advancement of technology, the evolution of cyber threats will also progress. The rapid expansion of Internet of Things (IoT) devices, coupled with the emergence of artificial intelligence (AI) and the growing interconnectedness of digital systems, will inevitably pose novel and complex obstacles for cybersecurity experts to overcome. Malicious individuals or groups will likely attempt to take advantage of these emerging technologies for their malicious intentions, thereby necessitating the development of innovative defensive strategies. Simultaneously, there exist opportunities to alleviate the risks presented by cyber threats through the means of collaboration, education, and technological innovation. Public-private partnerships have the potential to facilitate the exchange of information and enhance coordination among government agencies, private enterprises, and cybersecurity researchers. Investing in research and development has the potential to result in the development of innovative defensive technologies that are capable of effectively detecting and neutralizing emerging threats.

Importance of Cybersecurity Measures

Amidst the rapid digitization of our society, where technology has become deeply ingrained in various facets of our daily existence, the issue of cybersecurity has risen to the forefront as a matter of utmost importance. The significance of cybersecurity measures cannot be overstated, as they serve a crucial function in protecting individuals, businesses, and governments from a diverse range of cyber threats. The potential ramifications of insufficient cybersecurity are significant and wide-ranging, encompassing financial fraud, identity theft, espionage, and cyber warfare. Consequently, the implementation of robust cybersecurity measures is of utmost importance to safeguard our digital infrastructure and maintain confidence in the online ecosystem. The field of cybersecurity encompasses a wide array of practices, technologies, and processes that are specifically developed to safeguard against malicious cyber activities. The aforementioned activities encompass unauthorized access to sensitive information, disruption of essential services, and the exploitation of vulnerabilities in computer systems and networks. Considering the interconnectedness of the digital landscape, it is important to acknowledge that cyber threats can emerge from a multitude of origins, such as hackers, criminal syndicates, nation-states, and even individuals within an organization who may be dissatisfied. To effectively address the ongoing threat of cyber-attacks, both organizations and individuals must maintain a high level of vigilance and take proactive measures in their cybersecurity strategies.

One of the core tenets of cybersecurity is the implementation of preventive measures. It entails the implementation of measures to proactively identify and mitigate potential threats before they have the chance to cause any harm. As an illustration, organizations implement firewalls, intrusion detection systems, and antivirus software to effectively monitor and prevent suspicious network traffic and malware. Likewise, individuals can enhance their security by employing robust and distinctive passwords, activating two-factor authentication, and ensuring that their software remains current by installing the most recent security patches. By embracing a proactive approach, organizations have the potential to greatly mitigate their vulnerability to cyber-attacks.

Nevertheless, relying solely on prevention measures is inadequate when it comes to effectively mitigating the ever-changing threat landscape. The inclusion of both detection and response capabilities is of utmost importance in the realm of cybersecurity, as they are integral components of an effective security strategy. Notwithstanding our utmost endeavors to mitigate breaches, resolute adversaries may still discover means to infiltrate our fortifications. Hence, organizations must allocate resources towards the acquisition of cutting-edge technologies and the implementation of efficient processes that facilitate the prompt identification of security incidents and the subsequent execution of timely countermeasures to minimize their adverse effects. One potential course of action is to implement sophisticated threat detection tools, establish dedicated incident response teams, and regularly perform comprehensive security assessments to detect and mitigate vulnerabilities.

Moreover, it is important to note that cybersecurity extends beyond technical aspects and encompasses various human factors and organizational culture. Research findings indicate that a notable proportion of security breaches can be ascribed to human error, including actions such as clicking on phishing links or unintentionally revealing confidential information. Hence, it is of utmost importance to elevate consciousness and cultivate a climate of security awareness among the workforce. One way to accomplish this is by implementing continuous training and educational initiatives that provide individuals with knowledge about prevalent cyber threats and effective strategies for safeguarding sensitive data. In addition, fostering collaboration and promoting information sharing are fundamental components of a robust cybersecurity framework. The impact of cyber threats is not limited by geographical or sector-specific boundaries; rather, it can potentially disrupt organizations of any scale and across diverse industries. Consequently, the act of exchanging threat intelligence and implementing best practices can significantly enhance the overall defense against cyber-attacks. Collaboration between organizations, facilitated by public-private partnerships, industry alliances, and information-sharing forums, allows for the improvement of cybersecurity measures and the ability to respond more efficiently to emerging threats. Cybersecurity encompasses not only proactive defense measures but also incident response and recovery efforts. Notwithstanding our utmost endeavors to mitigate breaches, security incidents can transpire. Consequently, organizations must establish comprehensive incident response plans to effectively manage, examine, and resolve security breaches promptly. It is imperative to establish well-defined protocols to report incidents, as well as to effectively mobilize response teams and ensure seamless coordination with pertinent stakeholders, including law enforcement and regulatory authorities. Organizations can mitigate the impact of security breaches and accelerate the restoration of normal operations by implementing effective incident response capabilities.

Moreover, the significance of cybersecurity transcends the domain of business and personal privacy, encompassing substantial ramifications for national security and geopolitical stability. Amidst the current landscape characterized by the growing utilization of cyber-attacks for purposes of espionage, sabotage, and coercion, the imperative of safeguarding the durability of vital infrastructure and countering cyber threats has ascended to the forefront of governmental agendas worldwide. The aforementioned circumstances have resulted in the emergence of cybersecurity strategies, frameworks, and international cooperation initiatives that are designed to bolster cyber defense capabilities and foster the adoption of responsible norms in the realm of cyberspace. In addition, the exponential growth of Internet of Things (IoT) devices and the widespread implementation of cloud computing and artificial intelligence (AI) technologies have presented novel obstacles and intricacies within the realm of cybersecurity. The security features of IoT devices, such as smart home appliances and industrial control systems, are often inadequate, leaving them vulnerable to exploitation by cybercriminals. Moreover, the growing dependence on cloud services and AI algorithms presents novel avenues for potential exploitation by adversaries, thereby introducing new attack vectors and vulnerabilities. Thus, it is imperative to adopt a comprehensive approach to cybersecurity to effectively mitigate these emerging threats. This approach should encompass not only technological advancements but also regulatory oversight.

Key concepts and terminologies

Cybersecurity has emerged as an essential component of our modern digital era, encompassing a wide range of concepts and terminologies designed to protect our digital assets from malicious individuals. Within this extensive examination, we shall delve into the foundational principles and terminologies that delineate the world of cybersecurity, thereby offering lucidity and a profound understanding of this pivotal domain.

Analysis of Threats and Vulnerabilities

- **Threats**: Threats encompass any conceivable risks to information systems, encompassing but not limited to viruses, malware, hackers, and natural disasters.
- **Vulnerabilities**: Weaknesses within a system that can potentially be exploited by threats to compromise the security of data or operations.

Analysis of Potential Attack Vectors

- **Attack Vector**: An attack vector refers to the specified path or method that an attacker utilizes to gain unauthorized access to a computer system, network, or application.
- **Common Attack Vectors**: Common attack vectors include phishing, malware, social engineering, brute force attacks, and zero-day exploits.

Exploring Defense Mechanisms

- **Firewalls**: Firewalls are network security devices that are designed to monitor and control both incoming and outgoing network traffic. They do this by implementing predetermined security rules, which help to ensure that only authorized traffic is allowed to pass through the network. By acting as a barrier between the internal network and external networks, firewalls play a crucial role in protecting against unauthorized access and potential security threats.
- **Intrusion Detection Systems (IDS):** They are software or hardware solutions specifically developed to identify and promptly respond to unauthorized access attempts.

- **Encryption**: Encryption is the method used to encode information to render it unreadable without the appropriate decryption key.

Cybersecurity Frameworks

The NIST Cybersecurity Framework

- **NIST**: The acronym NIST stands for the National Institute of Standards and Technology.
- **Framework Core:** The Framework Core provides a structured approach for organizing cybersecurity activities, encompassing functions, categories, and subcategories.
- **Implementation Tiers:** The Implementation Tiers refer to the categorization of cybersecurity risk management practices based on their level of rigor and sophistication.

ISO/IEC 27001

- **ISO/IEC:** The acronym ISO/IEC stands for the International Organization for Standardization/International Electrotechnical Commission.
- **The Information Security Management System (ISMS):** This is a comprehensive and structured framework designed to effectively manage and protect sensitive company information.
- **Risk Management:** The process of identifying, assessing, and prioritizing risks, and then strategically allocating resources to minimize, monitor, and control the likelihood and consequences of adverse events.

Cybersecurity Threats and Trends

Ransomware

- **Ransomware**: Ransomware is a type of malicious software that is designed to encrypt files and then demand payment to release them.
- **Double Extortion**: The double extortion tactic refers to a method employed by ransomware operators, which entails the encryption of data and the subsequent threat to disclose the stolen information unless the demanded ransom is paid.

Advanced Persistent Threats (APTs)

- **APTs**: APTs, also known as Advanced Persistent Threats, are highly sophisticated and prolonged cyberattacks carried out by well-organized threat actors.
- **Attribution**: The process of attributing cyberattacks involves the identification of individuals or groups responsible for such activities. This task can be particularly challenging due to the use of advanced techniques aimed at concealing identities.

Internet of Things (IoT) security

- **IoT**: The Internet of Things (IoT) refers to a network of interconnected devices that can collect and exchange data.

- **Security Challenges:** Security challenges include weak authentication, lack of encryption, and susceptibility to botnet attacks resulting from insecure device configurations.

Compliance and Regulation

The General Data Protection Regulation (GDPR)

- **GDPR**: The General Data Protection Regulation (GDPR) is a regulation established by the European Union to safeguard the personal data and privacy of European Union citizens.
- **Key Principles**: The key principles that should be followed in data processing are lawfulness, fairness, and transparency. Additionally, it is important to implement measures for data minimization, accuracy, and accountability.

The Health Insurance Portability and Accountability Act (HIPAA)

- **HIPAA**: The Health Insurance Portability and Accountability Act (HIPAA) is a United States legislation that governs the security and privacy of healthcare information.
- **Protected Health Information (PHI):** The term "**Protected Health Information (PHI)**" refers to any health information that is individually identifiable and is transmitted or maintained by a covered entity or its business associates.

Emerging Technologies in Cybersecurity

Artificial Intelligence (AI)

- **AI**: Artificial Intelligence (AI) refers to the simulation of human intelligence processes by machines. This includes the ability to learn, reason, and self-correct.
- **AI in Cybersecurity**: Artificial Intelligence (AI) plays a crucial role in the field of cybersecurity. It is used for various purposes such as threat detection, anomaly detection, and automated response to security incidents.

Blockchain Technology

- **Blockchain**: The blockchain is a decentralized and distributed ledger technology that is used to record transactions across multiple computers.
- **Security Benefits:** The security benefits of this system are significant. The use of immutable record-keeping, cryptographic hashing, and decentralized consensus mechanisms greatly enhance data integrity and provide resilience against tampering.

The World without Cybersecurity

It is pertinent to note that individuals can be considered the most vulnerable link due to their unpredictable nature and complex combination of intentions, weaknesses, and beliefs. Undoubtedly, even the most robust system can be compromised through the implementation of social engineering tactics. There is no foolproof solution to mitigate the risks posed by insecure networks and firewalls when a client falls victim to phishing emails or social engineering tactics, such as divulging their passwords to individuals falsely claiming to represent the client relations department of a service provider.

The utilization of automation also emphasizes singular points of vulnerability, which could yield significant consequences if strategically targeted within communication and transportation infrastructures. With the increasing popularity of driverless cars, it is important to consider the potential consequences of developing automated products without prioritizing cybersecurity. In this case study, we will explore the possible outcomes that may arise from this oversight. In the foreseeable future, society will likely be governed by an automated transportation system encompassing various modes such as cars, trains, and buses. Additionally, aerial drones will be deployed to oversee crime prevention and identify any potential infrastructure malfunctions. An advantage to be considered is that this technological advancement will lead to increased efficiency by eliminating traffic congestion. Anticipated outcomes include a reduction in pollution levels due to the adoption of electric vehicle (EV) systems, resulting in decreased reliance on traditional fuel sources. Additionally, the implementation of EV technology is expected to significantly lower transportation costs, potentially leading to a complete elimination of such expenses. In the event of a worst-case scenario, it is possible for a cyberattack to compromise the entirety of the system. The potential disruption of the transportation network's coordinating systems could result in a complete cessation of operations throughout the city.

This would impede the commuting of workers, thereby causing a significant decline in productivity. Individuals reliant on life support systems will undoubtedly experience significant distress, as will those who depend on daily services to uphold their desired quality of life. In the absence of vital services, a state of disorder would swiftly follow, as individuals would face difficulties in meeting their basic needs and a sense of panic would ensue. The potential for the city to be subjected to foreign influence without the need for physical coercion is a matter of concern, as the ease with which such influence can be exerted is alarming. This concept presents a thought-provoking dystopian theory that sheds light on the direction in which society is progressing, emphasizing the imperative need to prioritize cybersecurity above all other considerations. It is worth considering the impact of the internet, as it has facilitated the emergence of novel business models that have significantly influenced global operations. Despite the profitability of search engines, social media, and ordering platforms as prominent online businesses, cybercrime surpasses them all. This observation highlights the significant profitability of fraudulent activities, as they thrive and exploit the lack of awareness among the vast majority of the 3.4 billion global users.

An Exploration of Threats

Cybercrime encompasses a range of activities, including denial-of-service attacks targeting websites, blackmail, unauthorized intrusion into computer systems, and sabotage. The potential threats include the integration of ransomware, malware, spyware, and alterations to the physical devices. It is unsurprising that the scope of attacks is extensive and exacerbated by the attack surface, which quantifies the vulnerabilities introduced by both hardware and software. If a hacking theme is effective on Apple devices and all members of the organization possess a device from the same company, be it an iPad, iPhone, or Macbook, it can be inferred that the potential attack surface is limited to a few individuals, or possibly even more. The number of employees can vary significantly, depending on the size of the company. From a different perspective, if any individual possessing an Apple device were to be exposed to potential threats on a worldwide scale, the potential target audience would encompass a significant number of individuals, potentially reaching millions. It should be noted that both programming and equipment can provide multiple vectors for potential attacks. For instance, an iPhone may possess various vulnerabilities, each of which has the potential to be exploited. Multiple methods can be employed to gain access to a computing device. The legal consideration is exemplified by the method employed to gain unauthorized access to the mobile devices of individuals involved in criminal activities. Their actions are justified by the principle of promoting the greater good, specifically the safety and well-being of the majority of citizens.

One can now comprehend the extent of damage that hacking can inflict on integrated systems, such as those related to power and transportation. In this particular scenario, the attacks exhibit a higher degree of focus, targeting specific industries. Consequently, the resulting consequences are significantly more severe. Disrupting the operation of the electrical grid, for instance, can potentially result in life-threatening ramifications. Observing it directly is not feasible, as it resides within the intricate infrastructure of fiber-optic networks and switches that permeate the internet. Nevertheless, cyber-attacks are occurring ubiquitously, including at this very moment. The modem in your residence, which provides internet connectivity, consistently defends against incoming queries aimed at verifying the availability of open ports associated with the assigned IP address. These refer to the virtual addresses that facilitate the communication of software to and from the network and the computers. Based on the assessments conducted by network security and administration firm Fortinet, it has been observed that a significant number of attacks, approximately 500,000, are consistently targeted toward its servers. That is one of the specialized organizations. The main concern revolves around the fact that virtually any aspect susceptible to technological advancements is bound to have vulnerabilities, which are constantly being tested by groups seeking to exploit these weaknesses for their gain. To fully comprehend the magnitude of challenges, the importance of cyber-security, and the associated legal concerns, it is imperative to thoroughly examine all possible avenues of attack.

Examining the Risks Addressed by Cybersecurity Measures

It is often stated that the significance of cybersecurity lies in its ability to thwart unauthorized access by hackers, thereby preventing data breaches and financial losses. However, this explanation fails to fully capture the extensive impact that cybersecurity has on maintaining the functionality of contemporary households, businesses, and even society at large, while also safeguarding individuals from potential physical harm. From a comprehensive perspective, the role of cybersecurity can be examined through various vantage points, each offering a distinct array of objectives. While the following lists may not be exhaustive, they serve as a valuable starting point for consideration and emphasize the significance of acquiring knowledge on how to ensure cybersecurity for yourself and your loved ones.

The objective of cybersecurity: The CIA Triad

Cybersecurity experts frequently articulate that the primary objective of cybersecurity is to guarantee the Confidentiality, Integrity, and Availability (CIA) of data, commonly referred to as the CIA Triad, with a playful nod to wordplay.

- Confidentiality is the practice of safeguarding information from unauthorized disclosure or access by individuals, organizations, or computer processes.
- The concept of integrity pertains to the assurance of data accuracy and completeness.

Accuracy refers to the assurance that data remains unaltered by unauthorized parties or technical glitches. The term "complete" pertains to data that remains intact without any portion being removed by unauthorized parties or technical glitches. Integrity encompasses the crucial aspect of nonrepudiation, which entails establishing and maintaining data in a manner that leaves no room for dispute regarding its authenticity or accuracy. The integrity of data can be compromised by cyberattacks that involve intercepting and modifying it before transmitting it to its intended destination. These types of attacks are commonly referred to as man-in-the-middle attacks.

- **Availability** pertains to the assurance that information, the systems employed for storage and processing, the communication mechanisms utilized for access and transmission, and all related security controls operate effectively to meet a predetermined benchmark, such as maintaining a 99.99 percent uptime. It is often observed that individuals who are not involved in the cybersecurity domain tend to perceive availability as a subordinate element of information security, following confidentiality and integrity. Indeed, the assurance of availability is a fundamental aspect of cybersecurity. However, accomplishing this task can be challenging, often more so than guaranteeing confidentiality or integrity. One of the reasons supporting this claim is that ensuring availability often necessitates the participation of numerous professionals who are not specialized in cybersecurity. This can pose a challenge akin to having an excessive number of individuals involved, particularly in larger organizations. Distributed denial-of-service (DDoS) attacks are a type of cyber-attack that aims to disrupt the availability of a targeted system or network. These attacks involve overwhelming the target with a flood of malicious traffic, rendering it unable to function properly. The primary objective of DDoS attacks is to undermine the availability of the targeted system or network, making it inaccessible to legitimate Additionally, it is important to take into consideration that cyber-attacks frequently employ significant amounts of illicitly obtained computing power and network bandwidth to carry out Distributed Denial of Service (DDoS) attacks. Conversely, those responsible for defending against such attacks and ensuring system availability are limited to utilizing only the comparatively modest amount of resources that they can financially afford.

The risks that cybersecurity addresses can also be conceptualized in a manner that more accurately captures the nuances of the human experience:

- **Privacy risks**: This refers to the potential dangers that arise from the potential loss of sufficient control over, or the improper use of, personal or other confidential information.
- **Financial risks:** The potential for financial losses resulting from unauthorized access and hacking activities. Financial losses can encompass both direct and indirect forms. Direct losses refer to instances like the unauthorized withdrawal of funds from an individual's bank account by a hacker who gained unauthorized access. On the other hand, indirect losses pertain to situations where a small business experiences a security breach, resulting in the loss of customer trust and subsequently, a decline in customer base.
- **Professional risks:** These are risks that can potentially impact one's professional career as a result of breaches or violations. Cybersecurity professionals face the potential risk of career damage in the event of a breach occurring under their supervision, particularly if it is determined to be a result of negligence. However, it is important to note that professionals from various other fields can also experience detrimental effects on their careers as a consequence of a breach. Chief-level executives have the potential to be terminated from their positions, while board members may face legal action in the form of lawsuits, among other possible consequences. Professional damage may also arise if hackers disclose confidential communications or data that portrays an individual unfavorably. This could include records indicating disciplinary action taken against someone for engaging in inappropriate behavior, or the exposure of an email containing objectionable content, among other possibilities.
- **Business risks:** These are risks that a business may face, which are similar to the professional risks that an individual may encounter. Internal documents were disclosed following a breach of Sony Pictures, revealing certain unfavorable aspects of the company's compensation practices.
- **Personal risks:** Numerous individuals store sensitive information on their electronic devices, ranging from explicit photographs to records of involvement in activities that may not be considered socially acceptable by individuals within their respective social circles. The unauthorized disclosure of such data has the potential to result in substantial

negative consequences for personal relationships. Similarly, the illicit acquisition of personal data can enable malevolent individuals to perpetrate identity theft, leading to a myriad of personal complications.

- **Physical danger risks**: This can arise from cyberattacks on critical infrastructure such as sewage treatment plants, utilities, and hospitals. Recent incidents have demonstrated the severe consequences of inadequate cybersecurity measures, including the potential endangerment of human lives.

Frequently Asked Questions

1. How do you define cybersecurity?
2. What is the history of cybersecurity?
3. What are the key concepts and terminologies of cybersecurity?
4. What is the importance of cybersecurity measures?
5. What does it mean to work in the cybersecurity field?

CHAPTER TWO
GETTING TO KNOW COMMON CYBER ATTACKS

Overview

Chapter two talks about the common cyberattacks around the world and how you can identify the harmful ones that can cause damage to your cyberspace.

Damage-Dealing Attacks

Cyber attackers use various methods to carry out their malicious intentions and cause harm to their targets. This text highlights the potential harm that can be caused by such attacks. It emphasizes that the attackers aim to benefit themselves and cause damage to the victims, whether it be financial, military, political, physical, or in other ways.

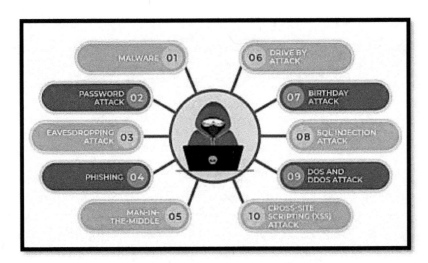

Various types of attacks can cause damage.
- DoS attacks
- Instances of distributed denial-of-service (DDoS) attacks
- Botnets and zombies
- Data destruction attacks

Denial-of-service (DoS) attacks

DoS describes how an attacker deliberately aims to disrupt or disable a computer or computer network by overwhelming it with excessive requests or data. As a result, the target becomes unable to handle legitimate requests effectively. The requests sent by the attacker are often seemingly innocent, such as a typical request to load a web page. In some instances, the requests deviate from the norm. They utilize their understanding of different protocols to send requests that enhance the impact of the attack. Denial-of-service attacks function by overloading computer systems' central processing units (CPUs) and memory, utilizing all the available network communications bandwidth, and exhausting networking infrastructure resources like routers.

Distributed denial-of-service (DDoS) attacks

DDoS attacks are a type of cyber-attack that can cause significant disruption to online services. They involve overwhelming a target system with a flood of traffic, rendering it unable to function properly. These attacks can be highly damaging and can impact a wide range of industries and organizations. A distributed denial-of-service (DDoS) attack occurs when numerous computers or connected devices from different locations inundate the target with requests, resulting in a denial of service. Over the past few years, there has been a significant shift in denial-of-service attacks. Nowadays, these attacks are predominantly distributed, with attackers using Internet-connected cameras and other devices as their primary attack vehicles, rather than traditional computers.

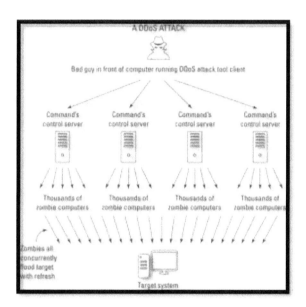

The objective of a DDoS attack is to disrupt the victim's online presence, and the reasons behind such actions can vary. Occasionally, the objective is monetary. Consider the potential harm that could be inflicted on an online retailer's business if a deceitful competitor were to disrupt their website during the busy Black Friday weekend. Picture a deceitful individual who strategically targets a prominent toy retailer, deliberately undermining their stock value, and orchestrating a disruptive DDoS attack just weeks before the holiday season. DDoS attacks continue to pose a significant and escalating danger. There are criminal enterprises that provide DDoS-for-hire services. These services are promoted on the dark web as a way to take down your competitor's websites for a fee. There are instances where DDoS launchers may be driven by political motivations, rather than financial gain. During an election season, corrupt politicians may attempt to sabotage their opponents' websites, limiting their ability to communicate their messages and receive online campaign contributions. Some hacktivists resort to launching DDoS attacks to bring down websites, claiming it as an act of "justice." For instance, they may target law enforcement sites following incidents where unarmed individuals are killed during altercations with the police. According to a 2017 study by Kaspersky Lab and B2B International, a significant number of companies worldwide, who have fallen victim to a DDoS attack, have expressed suspicions that their competitors might have played a role.

DDoS attacks have a considerable impact on individuals in three distinct ways:

- A DDoS attack on a local network can cause a considerable decrease in Internet access speed for all users on that network. At times, these attacks can significantly slow down connectivity, causing connections to fail due to session timeout settings. This means that the systems terminate connections when requests take longer to receive responses than the maximum permissible threshold.
- A DDoS attack has the potential to make a website inaccessible, which can be quite frustrating for users. On October 21, 2016, numerous users experienced difficulties accessing multiple well-known websites, such as Twitter, PayPal, CNN, HBO Now, The Guardian, and many others. This was caused by a significant DDoS attack targeting a third-party provider responsible for various technical services for these sites and more.

Performing online banking transactions at the last minute can be risky due to the potential for site inaccessibility. One reason for this is the occurrence of DDoS attacks, which can render the site unavailable.

- Users can be redirected to one site instead of another due to a DDoS attack. This action of making one site unavailable can have significant consequences. Internet users seeking specific information may turn to alternative sites, which can lead to the spread of misinformation or hinder access to diverse perspectives on important issues. DDoS attacks can serve as a potent tool for silencing dissenting opinions, albeit only in the short term.

Botnets and zombies

Botnets are commonly used in DDoS attacks. Botnets consist of computers that have been compromised by hackers and are controlled remotely to carry out tasks without the knowledge of their rightful owners. This passage highlights the potential actions of criminals who manage to infect a large number of computers with malware. These infected machines, often referred to as zombies, can be utilized by criminals to overwhelm a target server or server farm by generating numerous requests simultaneously.

Data destruction attacks

Occasionally, malicious individuals have intentions beyond temporarily disabling a party by inundating it with requests. Their objective may involve causing harm to the victim by destroying or corrupting their information and/or information systems. A criminal might attempt to delete a user's data using a data destruction attack, such as when the user refuses to comply with the demands of a ransomware ransom. Naturally, the motivations behind launching DDoS attacks (as discussed earlier) are also potential motivations for hackers to target and destroy someone's data. Wiper attacks are sophisticated data destruction techniques employed by criminals to completely wipe out the data on a victim's hard drive or SSD, making it extremely challenging, if not impossible, to retrieve the lost information. In simple terms, if the victim doesn't have backups, losing access to all the data and software previously stored on the attacked device is highly probable when it gets wiped by a wiper. The Internet poses a significant risk by enabling mischievous individuals to easily impersonate others. In the pre-Internet era, criminals faced significant challenges when it came to impersonating banks or stores and deceiving people into giving away their money in exchange for false promises of interest or goods. The rise of the Internet has provided scammers with an unprecedented tool to deceive unsuspecting individuals, surpassing the effectiveness of traditional methods such as physical mail and telephone calls. It is surprisingly easy to create a website that closely resembles the official website of a bank, store, or government agency. It can be accomplished in a matter of minutes. The abundance of domain names that closely resemble legitimate ones provides criminals with ample opportunities to deceive unsuspecting individuals. This allows them to create fake websites that appear genuine, laying the foundation for online impersonation.

Phishing

The act of phishing involves deceiving individuals by pretending to be a reliable source and persuading them to take certain actions. As an illustration, a criminal might send an email that seems to be from a well-known bank, requesting recipients to click on a link to reset their passwords due to a potential data breach. The link redirects users to a deceptive website that mimics the bank's official page, cleverly designed by the criminal. The criminal utilizes the fraudulent website to gather usernames and passwords for the banking site.

Spear phishing

Phishing attacks that are carefully crafted and directed at specific individuals, businesses, or organizations are known as spear phishing. To gain access to a specific company's email system, a criminal may send tailored emails to targeted individuals within the organization. Frequently, individuals who engage in spear phishing conduct thorough online research on their targets and exploit excessive personal information shared on social media to create emails that appear highly authentic. Take this email as an example, which is usually much more persuasive: "**Kindly access the mail server and proceed with resetting your password**." *Hey, just wanted to let you know that I'll be boarding my flight in ten minutes. Could you kindly log in to the Exchange server and verify the details of my upcoming meeting? I'm having trouble accessing it for some reason. Feel free to give me a call for security purposes, but if you're unable to reach me, please proceed to gather the information and send it to me via email. I'll be boarding a flight shortly.*

CEO fraud

The concept of CEO fraud is comparable to spear phishing (as discussed earlier) where a criminal pretends to be the CEO or another high-ranking executive of a specific company. However, instead of requesting login credentials, the impersonator may instruct the recipient to take direct action, without the intention of capturing usernames and passwords or similar information. For instance, a common tactic used by criminals involves sending an email to the company's CFO, directing them to make a wire payment to a newly introduced vendor, or forwarding all the organization's W2 forms to the email address of the firm's accountant. CEO fraud can result in substantial gains for criminals and can make employees who fall victim to these scams appear less capable. Consequently, individuals who become victims of these scams frequently face termination from their employment. CEO fraud saw a surge during the COVID-19 pandemic due to the shift to remote work, making it more challenging for individuals to authenticate the legitimacy of communications compared to the pre-pandemic era.

Smishing

Smishing involves instances of phishing where attackers send their messages through text messages (SMS) instead of email. The objective could be to obtain usernames and passwords or deceive the user into installing malware.

Vishing

Phishing through voice calls, also known as vishing, involves using traditional telephone services to deceive individuals. It's unfortunate that criminals still resort to these tried and tested tactics to exploit people. Today, the majority of these calls are transmitted through Voice over Internet Protocol (VoIP) systems. However, scammers continue to reach out to people using traditional telephones, just as they have been doing for decades.

Pharming

Pharming involves deceptive attacks that mimic phishing attempts, but exploit distinct technical weaknesses in Internet-based routing. Similar to phishing attacks, pharming attacks involve the impersonation of a trusted entity that may genuinely request the potential victim to perform a specific action. Although, in pharming attacks, the method differs from tricking users into visiting a fake website. Instead, the attackers manipulate routing tables and other network infrastructure to redirect users who click on a link or enter the legitimate website's URL to a criminal's clone.

Tampering with Other People's Belongings: A Serious Matter

Occasionally, attackers have ulterior motives beyond simply disrupting an organization's operations. They aim to exploit these activities for their financial benefit. Criminals often achieve their goals by manipulating data either while it is being transmitted or while it is stored in the systems of their targets. This technique is commonly referred to as tampering. Imagine a scenario where a user of online banking instructs the bank to wire money to a specific account. However, in this case, a criminal manages to intercept the request and manipulates the routing and account number to their advantage. Another way a criminal can gain unauthorized access to a system is by hacking and manipulating information for their purposes. In the given scenario, consider a situation where a criminal manipulates the payment address linked to a specific recipient. As a result, when the Accounts Payable department proceeds with an online payment, the funds end up being sent to an incorrect destination, according to the payer's perspective. One can also consider the potential consequences of criminal tampering with an analyst's report on a specific stock before it is made public. The criminal could then strategically buy or sell stocks based on the release of the report, taking advantage of the expected but ultimately incorrect effects of the false information.

Interception: Captured in Transit

Information can be captured by attackers during transit, which is known as interception. When it comes to cybersecurity, transit typically occurs between computers or electronic devices. However, it can also involve interactions between humans and devices, like capturing spoken voice for a voice recognition system. Ensuring proper encryption of data is crucial to prevent any potential misuse by unauthorized parties. Additionally, data obtained directly from humans, like voice recordings, is often unable to be encrypted.

Man-in-the-middle attacks

A man-in-the-middle attack is a particular type of interception. The data interception occurs when the interceptor acts as a proxy between the sender and recipient, aiming to conceal the interception itself. In this case, proxying involves the interception of requests by a man-in-the-middle, who then transmits them to their intended destinations. The responses from those destinations are received and transmitted back to the sender, either in their original form or with modifications. The use of proxying by the man-in-the-middle makes it challenging for senders to detect that their communications are being intercepted. This is because they receive the expected responses when communicating with a server. As an illustration, a criminal could create a fraudulent bank website and intercept any data entered by unsuspecting individuals. This allows the criminal to respond with the same information that the legitimate bank would have provided. This type of proxying not only enables criminals to evade detection but also allows them to ensure they obtain the correct password without the user suspecting any abnormal activity during their online banking session. If a user enters an incorrect password, the criminal will be alerted to request the correct one.

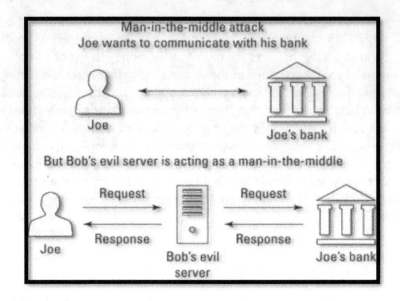

Data Theft

Cyberattacks often involve the unauthorized acquisition of the victim's data. Data theft is a serious concern that can impact individuals, businesses, or even government agencies. Attackers have various motives for engaging in such activities. Data theft can affect individuals, businesses, nonprofits, and governments alike.

Personal data theft

Individuals with malicious intent frequently attempt to pilfer personal information to discover valuable assets that can be converted into monetary gain. These assets may include:

- Data that can be exploited for identity theft or sold to individuals involved in identity theft
- Photos or health-related data that could be exploited or used for blackmail purposes
- Data that is unlawfully obtained and subsequently deleted from the user's device can then be held for ransom
- Lists of passwords that can be used to breach other systems
- Sensitive information regarding work-related matters that could potentially be exploited for illegal stock trading based on insider knowledge
- Details regarding future travel arrangements that could potentially be exploited for criminal purposes, such as targeting the victim's residence

Business data theft

Data stolen from businesses can be used by criminals for a variety of malicious intentions:

- **Making stock trades**: Criminals may also attempt to steal data to gain an unfair advantage by knowing a particular business's current and unreported quarter in advance. They then use that insider information to engage in illegal trading of stocks or options, potentially resulting in substantial financial gains.
- **Selling data to unscrupulous competitors**: Criminals can profit by selling stolen sales pipeline information, documents with details of upcoming products, or other sensitive data to competitors or employees who may use it to enhance their performance without their management's knowledge.
- **Leaking data to the media:** The exposure of sensitive information can lead to embarrassment for the victim and potentially impact their stock value.
- **Leaking data covered by privacy regulations:** The victim may face potential fines.
- **Recruiting employees**: Criminals who steal emails and discover communication between employees indicating dissatisfaction in their current positions can sell that information to other firms looking to hire employees with similar skills or knowledge of the competition's systems.
- **Using intellectual property without permission**: Individuals who unlawfully obtain the source code for computer software may be able to evade the payment of licensing fees to the rightful owner of the software. Design documents that are taken by parties without proper authorization can result in significant cost savings, potentially amounting to millions or even billions of dollars, by avoiding the expenses of research and development. To learn more about the impact of this kind of theft, check out the sidebar titled "How a cyber-breach cost one company $1 billion without 1 cent being stolen" located nearby.

Data exfiltration

The concept of data exfiltration may seem complex, but it essentially involves the unauthorized transfer of data from one system to another. This can be achieved through malware, automated methods, or manual commands issued to a remote computer. Whenever there is a data breach and criminals manage to copy sensitive data, it is considered an instance of data exfiltration. The impact of data leaks can be significant, affecting customer confidence, trust in government entities, confidentiality of proprietary information, and even national security.

Unauthorized access

Account authentication information that is known by someone other than you is referred to as compromised credentials. This includes your username and/or password. The act of abusing compromised credentials typically involves a criminal exploiting a login and password combination acquired from a cybersecurity breach. This allows them to gain unauthorized access to a system and carry out another breach. Attacks involving compromised credentials are quite common, as criminals are well aware that many people tend to reuse their login username/password combinations. In addition, the misuse of one employee's credentials by another employee, whether for malicious or non-malicious intentions, is also considered a form of such an attack.

Forced policy violations

This type of attack occurs when a user or device is compelled to violate cybersecurity policies, resulting in a forced policy violation attack.

Malware: Cyber Bombs That Infiltrate Your Devices

Malware, also known as malicious software, refers to software that deliberately causes harm to unsuspecting users without their knowledge. There are various types of malware, such as computer viruses, worms, Trojans, ransomware, scareware, spyware, cryptocurrency miners, adware, and other programs that aim to exploit computer resources for malicious purposes.

Viruses

Instances of malware known as computer viruses replicate by inserting their code into computer systems when executed. The insertion is commonly found in data files, such as rogue macros within a Word document, the specific section of hard drives or solid-state drives that house the code and data for booting a computer or disk (also referred to as boot sectors), or other computer programs. Computer viruses, much like their biological counterparts, can rapidly spread. However, to propagate, they require hosts to infect. The impact of computer viruses on their hosts can vary greatly, with some causing significant performance issues and others being relatively inconspicuous.

Worms

Computer worms are independent malware that can replicate themselves without relying on hosts to spread. Worms commonly spread through connections by taking advantage of security vulnerabilities on targeted computers and networks. Worms have the potential to cause harm by consuming network bandwidth, even without making any changes to systems or stealing data. Sluggish network connections can be quite frustrating for most people, as they prefer to have smooth and fast internal and Internet connections.

Trojans

Trojans are a type of malware that cleverly disguises itself as harmless software or hides within legitimate applications or digital data. They take their name from the infamous Trojan horse of history. Trojans are commonly distributed through social engineering tactics, such as deceiving individuals into clicking on links, downloading apps, or opening email attachments. Trojans, in contrast to viruses and worms, do not spread on their own through technology. Instead, they exploit the actions or errors made by humans.

Ransomware

Ransomware is a type of malicious software that unfortunately requires victims to pay a ransom to avoid potential harm caused by criminals. Ransomware commonly encrypts user files and issues threats to delete the encryption key unless a ransom is paid promptly. However, there are also instances where criminals steal user data and blackmail victims by threatening to publish it online unless a ransom is paid. The files stolen by certain types of ransomware are not just encrypted, but permanently taken from users' computers. This malicious tactic leaves users with no options for data recovery unless they choose to pay the ransom. Ransomware is commonly delivered to victims through various methods, including Trojans, viruses, and even worms, which have been utilized by criminals to successfully spread this malicious software. Criminals have become increasingly sophisticated in their approach, developing targeted ransomware campaigns that exploit their understanding of a target's valuable data and their ability to pay ransom.

Scareware

Scareware is a type of malware that manipulates individuals into taking certain actions through fear tactics. A common example is malware that frightens individuals into purchasing security software. The user receives a notification on their device stating that it has been infected with a virus and recommends a specific security package to remove it.

Spyware

Spyware is a type of software that secretly gathers information from a device without the user's consent. The spyware can capture various types of data, such as keystrokes, video, audio, and screen images. Understanding the distinction between spyware and invasive programs is crucial. Legitimate businesses are using certain technologies that, although invasive, do not qualify as malware. These technologies could potentially be classified as spyware if users were not informed about their online tracking. This category of non-spyware that also spies encompasses beacons that verify if a user has accessed a specific web page, as well as tracking cookies that are installed by websites or apps. There is ongoing debate among experts regarding the classification of software that monitors a smartphone's location even when the app is not in use by the user. This definition encompasses well-known apps like Uber, which some argue can be considered as non-spyware that also spies.

Cryptocurrency miners

Cryptocurrency miners, also known as crypto miners, are a type of malware that takes control of infected devices without the knowledge or consent of their owners. These malicious programs exploit the device's processing power (CPU cycles) to solve complex mathematical problems, generating new units of a specific cryptocurrency. The criminals behind the malware then reap the rewards of this illicit activity. In 2017, the number of cryptocurrency miners skyrocketed due to the surge in cryptocurrency values. Despite the subsequent drop in price levels, the miners remain widespread. Once criminals have invested in creating the miners, they find it cost-effective to continue deploying them. As cryptocurrency prices started to increase in 2019, new strains of crypto-miners emerged, including ones that specifically target Android smartphones. Cryptominers are often preferred by lower-level cybercriminals. Although each miner may only provide minimal payment to the attacker, miners can be easily acquired and used to directly profit from cyberattacks, without the need for additional steps or complex command and control systems.

Adware

Adware is a type of software that generates revenue by displaying online advertisements on a device. This text highlights the distinction between adware that is considered malware, as it is installed without the user's permission, and adware that is a legitimate component of software, which users may knowingly install as part of a free, ad-supported package.

Blended malware

Malware that is blended combines various types of malware technology to carry out attacks. This includes incorporating features from Trojans, worms, and viruses. Blended malware can be highly sophisticated and is typically the work of skilled attackers.

Zero-day malware

Newly discovered malware, known as zero-day malware, takes advantage of vulnerabilities that were previously unknown to the public or the technology vendor. This type of malware can be particularly powerful and dangerous. Developing zero-day malware regularly demands substantial resources and development efforts. It tends to be on the pricier side and is typically created by cyber armies of nation-states rather than other hackers. It is not uncommon for commercial purveyors to demand exorbitant prices, often exceeding $1 million, for a single exploit.

Fake malware on computers

Surprisingly, certain attackers don't even make the effort to hack computers. However, they simply send messages to potential victims, claiming that their computers are infected. To restore security to their devices, the targeted individuals are required to pay a fee or buy specific security software. Occasionally, wrongdoers can convey their messages through a pop-up window, while other times they opt for a more straightforward approach by sending them via email.

Malicious software targeting mobile devices

Malicious software is unfortunately prevalent on mobile devices, surpassing its presence on laptops and other computers. Due to certain technical factors, hacking mobile devices poses a greater challenge, leading many criminals to opt for a different approach. They often resort to feigning compromised devices to deceive potential victims into making payments. Some types of "**mobile device ransomware**" are designed to display ransomware-like demands on mobile devices, even if they haven't encrypted any data.

Phony security subscription renewal notifications

One example of a social-engineering attack that preys on people's commitment to online security involves the use of deceptive "*renewal notices*" sent by fraudulent anti-malware vendors. Be cautious when receiving an email claiming that your security software subscription is expiring. These emails may closely resemble legitimate ones, but it's important not to click any links or submit payment for renewal. Stay vigilant and verify the authenticity of such emails. It's no secret that this type of attack has become increasingly prevalent amid the COVID-19 pandemic. With more people working remotely and taking charge of their security software subscriptions, the risk has never been higher.

Attacks on Web Services: A Dangerous Threat

Cybersecurity professionals are constantly working to keep servers safe from the ever-evolving vulnerabilities that different types of attacks exploit. New weaknesses are regularly discovered, making their job a full-time commitment. Extensive literature can be found on this topic, but it is beyond the scope of this work to delve into it. You must grasp the fundamental concepts of server-based attacks as they can have a direct impact on you. Another form of attack is a poisoned web service attack or a poisoned web page attack. This type of attack involves an unauthorized individual gaining access to a web server and injecting malicious code. As a result, when users visit the affected pages, the server initiates attacks on them. As an illustration, a hacker could potentially infiltrate the web server responsible for serving www.abc123.com and alter the home page that users see when they visit the site, thereby inserting malware into the home page.

However, it is important to note that a hacker can poison web pages without even breaching a system! This site's lack of proper security measures can lead to a potential vulnerability. For instance, users can insert commands within their comments that, if carefully constructed, can be executed by browsers whenever the page with the comment is loaded. The criminal can insert a command that will execute a script on their website. This script can then capture the user's authentication credentials from the original site, as it is being called within one of the web pages on that site. This type of attack, known as cross-site scripting, remains a persistent problem despite efforts to address it for more than a decade.

Network Infrastructure Poisoning

Similar to web servers, various types of attacks exploit vulnerabilities in network infrastructure, and new weaknesses are frequently uncovered. However, it is important to have a good grasp of server-based attacks, as they can have a direct impact on you, especially in the case of poisoned web servers. As an illustration, individuals with malicious intent may take advantage of vulnerabilities to insert corrupted domain name system (DNS) data into a DNS server. The DNS serves as the Internet's directory, converting user-friendly addresses into computer-readable IP addresses. When you type in https://JosephSteinberg.com in your web browser, DNS will guide your connection to an address that consists of four numbers less than 256, separated by periods, like 104.18.45.53. A criminal can manipulate DNS tables to deceive a user's computer by providing it with an incorrect IP address. This type of attack has the potential to redirect a user's traffic to a computer chosen by the attacker, rather than the intended destination of the user. The criminal can take advantage of the diverted traffic by setting up a fake bank site on the server. They can then impersonate the bank that the user was originally trying to reach. This means that even if a user manually enters the bank's URL into their browser, they can still be tricked into falling for the scam after being redirected to the fraudulent site. (This form of attack is commonly referred to as DNS poisoning or pharming.)

Malvertising

Malvertising is a combination of malicious advertising, which involves using online ads to spread malware or launch cyberattacks. Online advertisements can be a potential vehicle for attackers, as many websites display ads served and managed by third-party networks that may contain links to various other third parties. Although some companies may have secure websites, they may still fail to take necessary precautions to prevent the distribution of problematic advertisements created and managed by third parties. The technique of malvertising enables criminals to discreetly place their content on well-known and highly-visited websites, reaching a large audience of security-conscious individuals who would not have encountered the criminal's content on a less reputable platform. In addition, websites typically generate revenue for their owners through ad clicks. As a result, website owners strategically position ads on their sites to maximize user engagement with the ads. Malvertising enables criminals to target large audiences through reputable websites without the need for hacking. The process of malvertising can vary. In some cases, users may need to click on the ads to become infected with malware. However, there are instances where no user interaction is necessary. Simply displaying the ad can lead to the infection of users' devices.

Drive-by downloads

Drive-by downloads can be misleadingly referred to as software that users unknowingly download without fully comprehending the consequences. Users may unintentionally download malware when visiting a compromised website that automatically infects their device without their knowledge. Drive-by downloads can sometimes catch users off guard, as they may not fully understand the potential consequences of downloading certain software. If a user encounters a web page claiming security vulnerability on their computer and instructing them to click a button labeled "**Download to install a security patch**," the user unwittingly grants authorization for the (malicious) download. This deception misleads the user into thinking the download serves a completely different purpose.

Password theft

There are various methods through which criminals can acquire passwords. There are two commonly used methods.

- **Thefts of password databases**: In the unfortunate event that a criminal manages to steal a password database from an online store, it is important to note that individuals whose passwords are present in the database may face the risk of their passwords being compromised. (Although the store may have implemented encryption for its passwords, there is still a possibility of a hash attack by the criminal. This means that passwords, especially those that are likely to be targeted first, could still be vulnerable. It is worth noting that stealing passwords remains the most prevalent method of compromising them.)
- **Social engineering attacks**: Social engineering attacks involve criminals deceiving individuals into performing actions they would not have done if they were aware of the deception. An instance of stealing a password through social engineering is when a criminal poses as a member of the target's tech support team and instructs the target to reset a specific password to a specific value for testing purposes following a security breach. The target, unaware of the trickery, complies with the request. (For further details, refer to the previous section on phishing.)
- **Credential attacks:** These attacks aim to gain unauthorized access to a system by using a valid username and password combination (or other required authentication information). There are four main categories that these attacks fall into:
1. **Brute force**: Criminals use automated tools to attempt every possible password until they find the correct one.
2. **Dictionary attacks**: Criminals employ automated tools to input every word in the dictionary into a site until they find the correct one.
3. **Calculated attacks**: Criminals exploit knowledge about a target to make educated guesses about their password. It is worth noting that criminals often target individuals by exploiting personal information, such as a person's mother's maiden name. This information can be easily obtained by examining common last names among a person's Facebook friends or from posts on social media platforms. (It's quite obvious when a Facebook post wishing a "Happy Mother's Day" is directed at someone with a different last name. It's a dead giveaway.)
4. **Blended attacks**: Certain attacks combine different techniques to enhance their effectiveness. For instance, they may use a database of common last names or employ a brute force attack that takes advantage of users' password formation patterns to improve efficiency.
- **Malware**: In the unfortunate event that criminals can infiltrate someone's device with malware, it has the potential to capture passwords.
- **Network sniffing**: When users send their password to a site without proper encryption on a public Wi-Fi network, there is a risk that a criminal using the same network can intercept and view that password while it's in transit. Additionally, other criminals

34

connected to networks along the path from the user to the site may also have the opportunity to see the password.

- **Credential stuffing** involves an individual trying to gain unauthorized access to a website by using stolen username and password combinations from another site.

Highlighting Maintenance Challenges

Computer system maintenance is a task of great importance. Software vendors frequently release updates that can potentially affect other programs running on a machine. However, certain patches must be installed promptly as they address software bugs that could potentially lead to security vulnerabilities. The ongoing struggle between security and adhering to maintenance procedures is a constant challenge, with security often coming up short. Consequently, most computers are not regularly updated. Even individuals who have enabled automatic updates on their devices may still not have the latest updates. This is because checks for updates are performed periodically rather than continuously, and not all software supports automatic updating. In addition, it is worth noting that updates to one software can sometimes lead to vulnerabilities in other software running on the same device.

Advanced Attacks

During a report of a major cyber breach, commentators often mention advanced attacks. Although there is no universally accepted definition of an advanced cyberattack, it is evident that certain attacks are more intricate and demand a higher level of technical expertise to execute. That being said, from a subjective standpoint, one might perceive any attack that necessitates a substantial investment in research and development for successful execution as being advanced. Naturally, the interpretation of what constitutes a significant investment can vary from person to person. There are instances where R&D expenditures reach staggering heights and the level of sophistication in attacks is so remarkable that there is almost unanimous consensus regarding their advanced nature. There is a difference of opinion among experts regarding the classification of zero-day attacks as advanced. Advanced attacks can occur in various forms, including opportunistic attacks, targeted attacks, or a combination of both. Opportunistic attacks involve targeting a large number of potential victims in the hopes of finding vulnerabilities that can be exploited. The attacker does not possess a predetermined list of targets. Instead, any vulnerable systems within reach become potential targets for the attack. The attacks resemble someone using a powerful shotgun in a crowded area, hoping that at least one pellet will successfully hit a vulnerable target. Targeted attacks focus on a specific party and involve employing various attack techniques until one successfully breaches the target. Further attacks may be initiated later on to navigate through the target's systems.

Opportunistic attacks

Most opportunistic attacks are driven by the desire for financial gain. Attackers are indifferent to whose systems they breach, as the end goal remains the same - to make money. In numerous instances, attackers may not bother concealing a breach, particularly once they've had the chance to profit from it. This could involve selling stolen lists of passwords or credit card numbers. Although not all opportunistic attacks are advanced, there are certainly some that are. There is a notable distinction between opportunistic attacks and targeted attacks.

Targeted attacks

When it comes to targeted attacks, breaching systems that are not on the target list is not considered a success, no matter how small. Take, for instance, the scenario where a Russian operative is tasked with hacking into the Democratic and Republican parties' email systems to obtain copies of all the emails stored on their servers. The success of this mission hinges solely on the operative's ability to accomplish these precise objectives. Even if the operative successfully steals $1 million from an online bank using the same hacking techniques employed against the targets, it will not transform a failure to breach the intended targets into even a minor triumph. In the case of a targeted attack, the attacker's primary objective is to bring down the website of a former employer they had conflicts with. In their perspective, attacking other websites would serve no purpose. Targeted attacks often use advanced attack methods to breach their targets, even if those parties have strong defenses. These methods may include exploiting vulnerabilities that are not yet known to the public or to the vendors responsible for fixing them. Advanced targeted attacks are usually executed by individuals or groups with significantly higher technical expertise compared to those who carry out opportunistic attacks. Targeted attacks typically have objectives beyond financial gain, such as discrete data theft or causing significant harm. After all, if one's objective is to maximize profits, why waste resources on a heavily fortified site? Adopt a strategic mindset and target the least protected, relevant websites.

Describing advanced threats used in targeted attacks as advanced persistent threats (APTs):

- **Advanced**: Uses sophisticated hacking techniques, possibly with substantial financial resources dedicated to research and development
- **Persistent**: Continuously explores various techniques to infiltrate a targeted system and doesn't give up easily, even if the initial target has strong security measures
- **Threat**: Poses a significant risk of causing severe harm

Blended (opportunistic and targeted) attacks

There is another type of advanced attack known as the opportunistic, semi-targeted attack. When it comes to stealing credit card numbers, criminals are not particularly concerned about which retailers they target. Whether it's Best Buy, Walmart, or Barnes & Noble, their main goal is to get their hands on as many active numbers as possible. The criminals' main focus is on obtaining credit card numbers, regardless of where they are stolen from. Simultaneously, launching attacks against sites that lack credit card data is an inefficient use of the attacker's time and resources.

Various Technical Attack Techniques

Although it may not be essential for the average person to delve into the intricacies of how technical cyberattacks exploit system vulnerabilities, it can be quite fascinating to grasp the fundamental concepts behind the popular methods employed by hackers. Here are some common methods that hackers use to breach and exploit technical systems.

Rootkits

Rootkits are software tool sets that enable attackers to carry out unauthorized activities at a privileged level on a compromised computer. The term **"root"** is used to describe the administrator account on UNIX systems. Rootkits often include features that aim to allow the attacker to maintain access without the authorized user or users of the compromised device being aware of it.

Brute-force attacks

Brute-force attacks involve an attacker attempting numerous possible values until their tools successfully guess the correct value. An example of a brute-force attack involves an attacker attempting to gain access to a user's account by systematically trying every possible password combination until the correct one is found. Alternatively, the attacker could attempt various decryption keys until they can successfully decrypt an encrypted message.

Injection attacks

Injection attacks occur when a system anticipates user input, but instead of receiving legitimate input, it is bombarded with malicious material such as code. This material can be executed by the system or distributed to others for execution. While it is true that coding applications correctly can help mitigate injection attacks, the unfortunate reality is that a significant number of systems remain susceptible to these attacks. Consequently, injection attacks continue to be a prevalent tool in the arsenal of hackers.

Cross-site scripting

XSS is a particular form of injection attack where an attacker inserts harmful code into a legitimate website. This code is then delivered to the user's device and executed when they visit the website through a web browser or app. The attacker can insert malicious code into the legitimate server due to the server's feature that allows users to submit material for display to other users. It is crucial to ensure that online user forums and social media platforms are adequately protected against cross-site scripting attacks to prevent any potential security breaches. Websites that allow users to comment on information, like news articles, are also quite popular. For instance, an XSS attack can occur when a hacker injects malicious code into a comment in a way that causes the code to be executed when another user's browser attempts to display the comment.

SQL injection

SQL injection attacks target relational databases by exploiting vulnerabilities in standard Structured Query Language (SQL) interfaces, which are commonly used to store and access data in computer systems. An SQL injection attack occurs when an attacker deliberately submits data to a system that contains SQL commands instead of regular data. As an illustration, suppose the system prompts the user to provide a user ID for searching purposes. If the attacker is familiar with the SQL command that the system is likely to use to search its database, they can exploit this by submitting a user ID that contains code to execute that command and then issuing another command to display all records in the database. If the system is not safeguarded against SQL injection, it may inadvertently carry out the attacker's intentions. The SQL injection attack may not result in the display of data, but the system's response can still inadvertently reveal valuable information about its handling of such attacks. This can potentially expose details about the system, database, and security measures in place, or lack thereof.

Session hijacking

Session hijacking occurs when an unauthorized individual gains control of a communication session between multiple parties. During an online banking session, if an attacker manages to intercept the connection between the user and their bank, they can continue the session with the attacker instead of the legitimate user. This is known as a successful session hijacking attack. The attacker gains complete control over the relevant system, effectively assuming the identity and privileges of the authenticated user. This allows them to carry out any actions that the legitimate user would have been authorized to do. Session hijacking is a common issue that arises when an application mishandles session management. This is particularly problematic when trust is placed in technical mechanisms that should not be relied upon to establish the authenticity of a session with a specific user.

Malformed URL attacks

Malformed URL attacks involve the manipulation of URLs to deceive users into thinking they are accessing a legitimate website when in reality; the URL contains special characters that enable malicious activities. The attacker can distribute the malicious URL through various channels, such as email, text messages, blog comments, or social media. There is another type of URL attack where an attacker deliberately creates a URL that includes certain elements to disrupt the functioning of the system being accessed.

Buffer overflow attacks

Buffer overflow attacks occur when an attacker intentionally overwhelms a system's memory buffer with data, causing it to overwrite other memory and potentially compromising the system's security. The system can be vulnerable to a carefully crafted buffer overflow input from an attacker. This input has the potential to overwrite the memory space where the system stores its commands.

Frequently Asked Questions

1. What are the different cyber-attack types?
2. How do you inflitrate your devices?
3. How do you maintain and stop cyber-attacks?
4. What are the different technical attack techniques?
5. What are opportunistic and targeted attacks?

CHAPTER THREE
CYBERATTACKERS AND THEIR COLORED HATS

Overview

In this chapter, you will learn about cyberattackers and their colored hats and how they can monetize their cyberattacks on businesses and individuals.

Cyberattackers categories

Cyber Attackers are commonly categorized according to their objectives:

- **Black hat hackers** engage in malicious activities, aiming to steal, manipulate, and/or destroy. Most people tend to associate hackers with the negative image of a black hat hacker.
- **White hat hackers** are ethical hackers who engage in hacking to evaluate, fix, and improve the security of systems and networks. These individuals are usually highly skilled computer security experts who specialize in penetration testing. They are often sought after by businesses and governments to identify vulnerabilities in their IT systems. White hat hackers are only considered legitimate if they have obtained explicit permission from the system owners before hacking into their systems.
- **Grey hat hackers** are individuals who may not have the same malicious intent as black hat hackers, but occasionally engage in unethical behavior or violate anti-hacking laws. The individuals who engage in the exploration of system vulnerabilities, without the consent of the system's owner, and responsibly disclose their findings without causing harm to any systems they examine, are commonly referred to as grey hat hackers. Some individuals in the hacking community engage in gray hat activities as a means of financial gain. For instance, when reporting vulnerabilities to system owners, they might propose fixing the issues in exchange for consulting fees. Some hackers are often categorized as black hat hackers, but it's worth noting that some of them fall into the grey hat category.
- Novices in the field of hacking, **green hat hackers** aspire to become experts. The position of green hats within the white-grey-black spectrum may change over time, just like their level of experience.

- **Blue hat hackers** are hired to thoroughly examine software for potential vulnerabilities before its release to the market.

It is important to focus on black and gray hat hackers as they pose the greatest threat to your cybersecurity and the safety of your loved ones.

Exploring the Monetization Strategies of Cybercriminals

Some cyberattackers have a motive for financial gain, although this is not true for all of them.

There are various methods through which cyberattackers can profit from their malicious activities:

- Instances of direct financial fraud
- Financial fraud through indirect means
- Ransomware
- Cryptominers

Direct financial fraud

There is a potential risk of hackers attempting to directly steal money through various attacks. As an illustration, hackers can install malware on individuals' computers, enabling them to intercept online banking sessions and manipulate the online banking server to transfer funds to their accounts. It's no secret that criminals are aware of the strong security measures in place for bank systems. As a result, many have shifted their focus to targeting systems that are not as well-defended. This is an example of how criminals have shifted their focus to capturing login credentials for systems that store credits. They target apps like coffee shop apps that allow users to store prepaid card values. By stealing the money from these accounts, they can use it to make purchases elsewhere. In addition, if criminals gain access to accounts of users with auto-refill capabilities enabled, they can repeatedly steal the value with each auto-reload. In addition, it is important to be aware that criminals may attempt to exploit individuals' frequent traveler accounts for their gain. They may try to transfer the accumulated points to different accounts, make unauthorized purchases, or acquire plane tickets and hotel rooms that they can sell to others in exchange for cash. Unfortunately, criminals can exploit credit card numbers, either by using them themselves or selling them to others who engage in fraudulent activities. There are various nuances to the concept of being direct; it's not simply a matter of black and white.

Indirect financial fraud

Cybercriminals who are more experienced tend to steer clear of cybercrimes that involve direct financial fraud. This is because these schemes usually result in smaller amounts of money and can be easily disrupted by the victims themselves, such as reversing fraudulent transactions or canceling orders made with stolen information. Additionally, these types of crimes carry a higher risk of getting caught. Alternatively, they might aim to acquire data that they can exploit for fraudulent purposes.

There are various instances of such offenses, which include:

- Engaging in the illicit trading of securities for personal gain
- Acquiring credit card, debit card, or other payment-related information without authorization
- Taking goods without permission
- Unauthorized acquisition of data

Profiting off illegal trading of securities

Illegal trading of securities, such as stocks, bonds, and options, can be a lucrative endeavor for cybercriminals.

They employ various methods to amass their fortunes:

- **Pump and dump**: Hackers infiltrate a company, pilfer its data, and manipulate the stock market by shorting the company's stock. They then release the stolen data online, causing the stock price to plummet. Seizing the opportunity, they repurchase the stock at a lower price to cover their short sale.
- **Misleading press releases and social media posts**: Unscrupulous individuals engage in the practice of purchasing or selling a company's stock, followed by the dissemination of misleading information through fake news or by gaining unauthorized access to the company's marketing systems or social media accounts. This allows them to issue false positive or negative news through the company's official channels.
- **Insider information**: Criminals may attempt to steal drafts of press releases from a public company's PR department to gain insight into any potential unexpected quarterly earnings announcements. When a dishonest individual discovers that a company is about to release significantly stronger numbers than anticipated by Wall Street, they may choose to acquire call options. These options grant the individual the right to buy the company's stock at a predetermined price, and their value can soar following such an announcement. In a similar scenario, when a company is on the verge of revealing unfavorable news, an individual with malicious intent may engage in short-selling the company's stock or acquiring put options. These options grant the individual the ability to sell the company's stock at a predetermined price. The value of these options can surge if the market price of the corresponding stock declines.

Discussions of indirect financial fraud of the aforementioned types are grounded in reality, supported by concrete evidence of criminals engaging in such behavior. These types of scams are frequently less risky for criminals compared to directly stealing money. Regulators find it challenging to detect such crimes in real-time, and reversing any relevant transactions is nearly impossible. Sophisticated cybercriminals see a potential gold mine in the lower risks of getting caught and the relatively high chances of success.

Stealing credit cards, debit cards, and other payment-related information

It is a common occurrence in news reports that criminals frequently target credit card or debit card numbers for theft. These numbers can be used by thieves to make purchases without any payment. The tactics used by criminals involve purchasing electronic gift cards, software serial numbers, or other assets that can be easily resold for cash. They may also opt to buy physical goods and services, having them delivered to vacant houses for convenient pick-up. Many criminals do not use the credit cards they acquire through theft. They sell the numbers on the dark web, specifically to criminals who can efficiently exploit the credit cards before fraud is reported and the cards are blocked.

Stealing goods

In addition to the types of theft mentioned earlier, certain criminals target valuable, small, liquid items like jewelry by seeking information about high-value orders. In certain instances, they intend to pilfer the items upon delivery to the recipients, rather than engaging in deceitful transactions.

Stealing data

Certain individuals engage in the act of stealing data to use it to commit a range of financial crimes. Some individuals engage in the act of stealing data to sell it or make it public. Data stolen from a business, for instance, can be highly valuable to a dishonest competitor.

Ransomware

Ransomware is a type of computer malware that maliciously restricts users from accessing their files, coercing them into paying a ransom to unscrupulous individuals or criminal organizations. This particular cyberattack has already resulted in criminals making billions of dollars and putting countless lives at risk by rendering hospital computer systems inaccessible to doctors. There have been instances where ransomware may have tragically resulted in premature or avoidable loss of life. The threat of ransomware continues to increase, as cybercriminals continuously enhance the technical capabilities and financial gains of their cyberweapons. Some criminals create ransomware intending to maximize their profits. They infect computers and then try to infiltrate connected networks and devices to locate the most valuable systems and data. Instead of seizing the data it initially comes across, the ransomware becomes active and blocks access to the most valuable information. It is widely known among criminals that the value of information to its owner directly influences the likelihood of a ransom being paid, as well as the potential maximum amount that can be obtained. Ransomware has become more and more elusive, managing to evade antivirus software and go undetected. In addition, the individuals behind ransomware often carry out deliberate attacks on specific targets whom they believe can afford to pay substantial ransom. It is widely known that criminals are aware of the higher likelihood of an average American paying a $200 ransom compared to someone living in China. In addition, they frequently focus on environments where being disconnected has severe repercussions. For instance, a hospital cannot afford to operate without its patient records system for an extended duration.

Cryptominers

In malware, a crypto miner is a type of software that cunningly hijacks a computer's resources to carry out intricate mathematical calculations required for generating fresh units of cryptocurrency. The currency generated is transferred to the criminal behind the crypto miner. Cryptominer malware variants often rely on networks of infected machines to carry out their mining operations. Cryptominers have become an attractive option for cybercriminals who lack the skills for targeted ransomware attacks. By generating money for criminals without involving their human victims, crypto miners offer a quick and easy way to monetize cyberattacks. Although the value of cryptocurrencies can be highly volatile, it is worth noting that certain cryptocurrency mining networks have been reported to generate over $30,000 per month for their operators.

Dealing with Non Malicious Threats: Not All Dangers Come From Attackers

While there are individuals who seek to exploit you, there are also those who have no malicious intentions. Nevertheless, these parties have the potential to unknowingly cause dangers that may surpass those presented by malicious actors.

Human error

Human error poses a significant cybersecurity risk for individuals, businesses, and government entities alike. Most of the significant breaches highlighted in the media in the past decade were enabled, to some extent, by human error. Hostile actors are well aware that human error is often necessary for them to succeed in their attacks.

The vulnerability of cybersecurity lies in humans

Why do humans frequently become the vulnerable link in the cybersecurity chain, leading to significant breaches due to their mistakes? The answer is straightforward. Think about the incredible progress that technology has made in the past few years. The prevalence of electronic devices in today's world is a stark contrast to their portrayal in science-fiction literature and films of the past. Technology has far exceeded expectations in numerous instances. Advancements in security technology have been significant over the years. Each year, a multitude of new products are introduced, along with numerous enhanced iterations of existing technologies. The advancement in intrusion detection technology today surpasses that of a decade ago to such an extent that classifying them as the same category of product offering is debatable. On the other hand, let's consider the human brain. The evolution of human brains occurred over tens of thousands of years, with no significant changes happening within a single human lifetime or even over several generations. Security technology progresses at a much faster pace than the human mind. In addition, with the continuous advancements in technology, individuals are frequently required to engage with and comprehend a wide range of intricate devices, systems, and software. Considering the inherent limitations of human beings, the probability of individuals making substantial errors tends to increase as time goes on. It is evident that the demand for intellectual capacity, driven by the progress of technology, is becoming more apparent even in everyday situations. Do you ever wonder how many passwords your grandparents had to remember when they were your age? How many did your parents require? How many do you require? How vulnerable were passwords to remote hacking and exploitation during your grandparents' time? Are your parents involved? And what about you? In today's complex work environment, the challenges are multiplied when individuals have to juggle working from home and overseeing their children's remote schooling. This situation increases the likelihood of human errors, whether it's due to interruptions during tasks or the absence of face-to-face communication with colleagues. It is crucial to understand and acknowledge that human error can significantly jeopardize your cybersecurity. Therefore, it is essential to take appropriate action to mitigate this risk.

Social engineering

In terms of information security, social engineering involves the manipulation of individuals' psychology to coax them into engaging in actions that they would typically avoid, actions that often have negative consequences for them.

Here are some instances of social engineering:

- Pretending to be a member of the IT department over the phone and deceiving someone into resetting their email password
- Sending deceptive emails
- Sending deceptive emails impersonating CEOs

The criminals behind social engineering attacks may have malicious intent, but those responsible for creating the vulnerability or causing the damage usually do so without any intention of harming the target. The user who resets their password in the first example is under the impression that they are assisting the IT department in resolving email issues, rather than unknowingly granting access to hackers into the mail system. Similarly, individuals who become victims of phishing or CEO fraud scams do not intend to assist the hackers who are targeting them. Various forms of human error can compromise cybersecurity, such as unintentionally deleting information, misconfiguring systems by mistake, unknowingly infecting a computer with malware, disabling security technologies by accident, and other innocent errors that can be exploited by criminals for their malicious activities. It is crucial to always acknowledge and recognize the undeniable presence and impact of human errors, including your own. We all make mistakes, including you and me. It's just a part of being human. It is crucial to thoroughly verify that everything is in order when it comes to important matters. It is important to thoroughly verify any potential social engineering attacks, even if there have been false alarms in the past. It's better to be safe than sorry.

External disasters

Cybersecurity involves ensuring the confidentiality, integrity, and availability of your data. External disasters pose a significant threat to availability, and can also indirectly impact the confidentiality and integrity of data. There are two categories of disasters: those that occur naturally and those that are caused by humans.

Natural disasters

Many individuals reside in regions that are susceptible to different types of natural disasters. Nature's wrath knows no bounds, wreaking havoc on computers and the precious data they hold. Hurricanes, tornados, floods, and fires can all leave a trail of destruction in their wake. Continuity planning and disaster recovery are included in the certification process for cybersecurity professionals. It is a fact that statistically speaking, the majority of individuals will come across and go through at least one type of natural disaster during their lifetime. It is crucial to plan to safeguard your systems and data from potential risks. It's no wonder that organizations that had well-prepared continuity plans in place fared significantly better than their unprepared counterparts when the COVID-19 pandemic struck and forced people to work remotely. Storing backups on hard drives at two different sites might not be the best approach, especially if both sites are basements in homes located within flood zones.

Pandemics

A specific type of natural disaster includes pandemics or other medical emergencies. It is evident from the events of 2020 that the outbreak of a highly contagious disease can lead to the abrupt closure of physical workplaces and schools, resulting in a rapid shift to online platforms. This transition, however, brings about various cybersecurity challenges.

Issues caused by human activity in the environment

Nature is not the sole contributor to the external problems we face. It is important to acknowledge that humans can trigger floods and fires, and unfortunately, the consequences of these man-made disasters can often surpass those that happen naturally. In addition, the availability of data and systems can be affected by various factors such as power outages, power spikes, protests, riots, strikes, terrorist attacks, Internet failures, and telecom disruptions. After the tragic events of 9/11, businesses faced the harsh reality of the importance of keeping backups outside the vicinity of their corresponding systems. Those who had backed up their data from systems located in New York's World Trade Center to systems in the nearby World Financial Center learned this lesson the hard way, as the World Financial Center remained inaccessible for an extended period following the destruction of the World Trade Center.

Cyberwarriors and cyberspies

Modern-day governments frequently possess formidable armies of cyberwarriors under their command. Teams like these often aim to uncover vulnerabilities in software products and systems, utilizing them for offensive purposes such as attacking and spying on adversaries, or even as a tool for law enforcement. However, there are risks involved for individuals and businesses when doing so. Although vulnerabilities are often kept secret by government agencies instead of being reported to the relevant vendors, this approach can leave citizens, enterprises, and other government entities vulnerable to attacks by adversaries who may also discover the same vulnerability. Furthermore, governments may utilize their teams of hackers to combat crime — or, in certain instances, exploit their cyber-resources to maintain authority over their citizens and uphold the ruling party's grip on power. The government in the United States implemented various programs of mass data collection that impacted law-abiding U.S. citizens, particularly in the aftermath of 9/11. There is a potential risk to U.S. citizens if any of the databases that were assembled were accessed by foreign powers, leading to various cyber-related issues. The risks associated with governments creating collections of data exploits are not merely hypothetical. It has come to light that in recent years, several highly potent cyberweapons, which are widely believed to have originated from a U.S. government intelligence agency, have emerged on the internet. These weapons were unlawfully obtained by an individual or group whose motives were in direct opposition to those of the agency. It is still uncertain whether those weapons were used against American interests by the individuals who stole them.

The ineffective Fair Credit Reporting Act

The Fair Credit Reporting Act (FCRA) is a set of laws that many Americans are familiar with. It was initially passed nearly half a century ago and has been updated multiple times. The FCRA governs the collection and handling of credit reports and the information contained within them. The FCRA was established to promote fairness and protect the accuracy and privacy of credit-related information.

The Fair Credit Reporting Act mandates that credit reporting bureaus are required to remove certain types of negative information from individuals' credit reports once specific periods have passed. It is important to note that if you fail to pay a credit card bill on time during your college years, it is actually illegal for the late payment to be included in your credit report and negatively impact your credit score when you seek a mortgage many years down the line. Even individuals who declare bankruptcy to make a fresh start can have their bankruptcy records expunged under the law. Starting over would lose its value if bankruptcy permanently hindered someone from having a fresh start. Today, though, several technology companies are undermining the protections of the FCRA. Is it easy for a bank's loan officer to locate online databases of court filings about bankruptcies through a basic Google search and subsequently extract relevant information for a potential borrower? Or is it possible to check if there are any foreclosure records linked to a name that matches the person applying for a loan? It only takes a few seconds to do either, and there are no legal restrictions on including older records in these databases. In the United States, there are also no laws preventing Google from displaying links to these databases when someone searches for the name of someone involved in such activities many years ago.

Expunged records are no longer expunged

The justice system has a range of laws that often provide young individuals with the opportunity to prevent minor offenses from appearing on their permanent criminal records. In addition, our laws grant judges the power to seal specific files and remove certain types of information from individuals' records. These laws are instrumental in providing individuals with a fresh start. It is widely recognized that many exceptional and valuable contributors to our society owe their success to these important safeguards. However, the effectiveness of these laws is called into question when a potential employer can easily uncover supposedly erased information with a simple Google search of a candidate's name. Google provides access to results from local police blotters and court logs that have been published in local newspapers and are now available in online archives. Individuals who were cited for minor offenses and subsequently had all charges dismissed may still face long-lasting professional and personal consequences, despite never being indicted, tried, or convicted of any offense.

Social Security numbers

In the past, it was a common practice to use Social Security numbers as identification numbers for college purposes. In the past, the world was quite different. As a result, some schools used Social Security numbers instead of students' names when posting grades, for privacy reasons. Indeed, without a doubt. Should all students who attended college in the 1970s, 1980s, or early 1990s have their Social Security numbers exposed to the public due to the online archiving of college materials from the pre-web era? In addition, certain parties rely on the last four digits of individuals' phone numbers for user authentication, a piece of information that can be easily obtained through a quick search on search engines like Google or Bing. Given the widespread awareness of the vulnerabilities resulting from past practices, one might question why the government continues to rely on Social Security numbers and handle them with the assumption of privacy. In addition, online archives of the church, synagogue, and other community newsletters frequently include birth announcements that provide detailed information such as the baby's name, the parents' names, and the hospital where the child was born, the date of birth, and even the names of the grandparents. Can a single announcement about security questions for a user of a computer system undermine multiple questions for a crook? These examples highlight the potential negative consequences of technological advancements on our privacy and cybersecurity, including the potential legal implications that can compromise established protective measures.

Social media platforms

Social media platforms pose significant risks to cybersecurity for technology businesses. Companies and their employees are at risk as cybercriminals are now scanning social media, often using automated tools, to gather information that can be used against them. Attackers use the information they discover to create various types of attacks, including those that involve the distribution of ransomware. As an illustration, they can create spear-phishing emails that are so convincing that employees are tricked into clicking on URLs that lead to websites delivering ransomware or opening attachments infected with ransomware. Virtual kidnapping scams have seen a significant increase in recent times. Criminals now exploit social media to gather information about potential victims, determining the perfect time to strike and who to target. They contact the families of individuals who are temporarily unreachable, demanding a ransom for the release of their claimed hostage.

Google's highly advanced computers

The verification process used by computer systems involves posing questions that only the rightful individuals would be able to answer accurately. When it comes to determining your current mortgage payment, there are several factors to consider. However, the authentication process is undermined by the all-knowing Google engine. The availability of information has significantly improved in recent years, with the ability to access a wealth of knowledge through a simple Google search. Unfortunately, the answers to security questions used by various websites to help authenticate users are easily accessible to criminals with just a click. The timing of entering the answer to security questions can vary across different websites. While some more advanced sites may consider a delayed response as incorrect, many sites do not have such restrictions. This lack of restrictions can potentially allow individuals with knowledge of using search engines like Google to bypass certain modern authentication systems.

Tracking the location of mobile devices

In addition, Google can analyze various types of data collected from Android phones, as well as its Maps and Waze applications. This likely includes a significant portion of the population in the Western World. It is worth noting that other app providers, who have access to location data and are installed on numerous devices, can also perform similar actions. This party's tracking of a person's location and duration of stay could potentially lead to the creation of a database with various malicious applications. These may include compromising knowledge-based authentication, enabling social engineering attacks, and undermining the confidentiality of classified projects, among other concerns. The security of the database is a major concern, as unauthorized individuals could potentially access or steal sensitive information, even if the company responsible for its creation has no ill intentions. This tracking also poses a threat to privacy. The information that Google collects includes data on individuals visiting chemotherapy facilities and their sleeping patterns. This data can be used to make sensitive extrapolations about individuals and their surroundings.

Protecting against These Attackers

It's crucial to recognize that achieving absolute cybersecurity is simply not possible. This misconception about the security of manual typewriters is quite common. However, it is important to note that even using a manual typewriter does not guarantee complete cyber security. Someone can decipher the content by carefully listening to the distinct sounds produced by the striking of each letter on the paper. Instead of striving for absolute cybersecurity, we should focus on achieving a level of cybersecurity that is sufficient. This means having a clear understanding of the existing risks, identifying the ones that are effectively addressed, and addressing the ones that remain. Some defenses may be effective against certain risks and attackers, but they may fall short when it comes to protecting against others. What might be sufficient for adequately protecting a home computer, for instance, may be grossly insufficient for safeguarding an online banking server. The security requirements for a cellphone used by the President of the United States to communicate with advisors are significantly higher compared to the cellphone used by an average sixth grader.

Frequently Asked Questions

1. What are the different categories of cyberattackers?
2. How do you defend against these cyber-attacks?
3. How do cyber criminals make their money?

CHAPTER FOUR
PROTECTION AGAINST CYBER ATTACKS

Overview

Chapter four discusses how best you can protect yourself and your internet-based business from cyber-attacks and the measures you should employ.

Understanding Your Current Cybersecurity Posture

Understanding what needs to be protected is crucial in enhancing your defense against cyberthreats. Once you have a solid understanding of that information, you can assess the necessary measures to ensure sufficient security and identify any potential areas that require attention.

It is important to take into account the data you possess, the individuals you need to safeguard it from, and the level of sensitivity it holds for you. What would be the outcome if, for instance, it was shared on the Internet for everyone to view? After considering the amount of time and money you're willing to invest, you can assess how much you're willing to allocate towards safeguarding it.

Threat to Computers

There are a few major types of potential problems that your home computers may encounter in terms of cybersecurity:

- **Breached**: It is possible that an unauthorized individual has gained access to your home computer and can utilize it in various ways. They may be able to view the contents of your computer, communicate with other machines, use it as a base to launch attacks on other computers, phones, and smart devices, extract cryptocurrency, access data on your network, and more.

- **Malware**: Just like human invaders, there's a computer-based attacker called malware that can be present on your home computer. This allows criminals to use your computer to do various things like accessing its contents, contacting other electronic devices, mining cryptocurrency, and more. Additionally, malware can read data from your network traffic and infect other computers on your network and beyond.
- **Using shared computers**: Sharing a computer with others, such as your significant other or children, can put your device at risk. Not everyone may practice the same level of cyber-hygiene as you do, which could lead to malware infections, hacking breaches, or unintentional damage to the device.
- **Connections to other networks and storage applications**: When your computer is connected to other networks through a virtual private network (VPN), there is a risk of network-borne malware or hackers from those networks targeting your network and local devices. There may be instances where comparable risks are present when running applications that establish connections between your computer and remote services, like remote storage systems.
- **Considerations for physical security risks**: The safety of your computer and its contents can be influenced by its physical location.

Your mobile devices

Mobile devices pose inherent risks from an information security standpoint due to their

- Being constantly connected to the Internet exposes us to the risks of a highly insecure, public network where hackers are known to lurk and cyberattacks frequently occur.
- Frequently contain substantial amounts of sensitive data
- Used for communication with various individuals and systems, including groups that may not always be reliable, through the Internet (which is inherently untrustworthy)
- Receiving inbound messages from unfamiliar parties, some of whom may have malicious intentions, is a possibility.
- Security software may not always be fully utilized due to limited resources, or you may be restricted to using pre-installed software that cannot be manually upgraded or modified to better suit your requirements.
- It is important to note that there is a risk of loss or theft.
- It is important to note that this item is susceptible to accidental damage or destruction.
- Frequently connect to insecure and untrusted Wi-Fi networks
- Items are frequently replaced without proper decommissioning when they are disposed of.
- Devices are frequently traded in for upgrades without undergoing proper decommissioning.

Your Internet of Things (IoT) devices

In recent years, the landscape of connected computing has undergone a significant transformation. In the not-so-distant past, the Internet was primarily accessed through traditional computers such as desktops, laptops, and servers, which served a wide range of computing needs. Today, though, we find ourselves in a completely different world where computers make up just a fraction of the connected devices. Today, a wide range of electronic devices, from smartphones to security cameras, refrigerators to cars, and even coffeemakers to exercise equipment, are equipped with powerful computers that are constantly connected to the Internet. The Internet of Things (IoT), or the network of connected devices, has experienced significant growth in recent years. However, the security measures implemented for these devices are often insufficient. IoT devices often lack the necessary security technology to protect themselves from potential breaches. Many systems, even when they are set up, often lack proper security configurations. The vulnerabilities of IoT devices can be exploited by hackers to engage in activities such as spying on individuals, stealing sensitive data, launching attacks on other systems or devices, initiating denial-of-service attacks on networks or devices, and causing various other types of harm.

Your networking tool

Networking equipment is vulnerable to hacking, which can result in the unauthorized rerouting of traffic, data breaches, cyber-attacks, and even internet access disruptions.

Your work environment

It's important to be aware of the potential risks that can arise from sensitive data in your work environment, including the actions of your colleagues. This scenario highlights the potential risks of connecting electronic devices to different networks, such as bringing them from work to home. In such cases, there is a possibility of malware and other issues spreading from your employer's or colleagues' devices to yours, and then further infecting other machines on your home network. Undoubtedly, the COVID-19 pandemic has resulted in the convergence of work and home environments, causing significant cybersecurity concerns.

Risk Identification

To effectively secure something, it is crucial to have a clear understanding of what exactly you are securing. Without this knowledge, attempting to secure an environment becomes an incredibly challenging, if not impossible, task. To ensure your security, it is crucial to have a clear understanding of the assets you possess, including both digital and physical formats, and identify what you aim to safeguard. The assets may or may not be in one location. It's worth noting that some or all of them might be in places that are not physically accessible to you. As an illustration, data can be stored in various cloud storage services like Google Drive, Apple iCloud, or Microsoft OneDrive. It is crucial to have a clear understanding of the risks associated with your assets.

Understanding Endpoints

A computer-enabled device that communicates with a network is known as an endpoint. The laptop functions as an endpoint when connected to the home network, while the smartphone acts as an endpoint when connected via Wi-Fi or cellular connection like 4G or 5G to the network of a cellular provider. Endpoints are referred to as such because they mark the conclusion of a communication path. Internet-based communications often traverse multiple nodes before reaching their destination, but once they reach the endpoint, the hopping ceases. Securing all endpoints is crucial due to the inherent risks they present. It is important to ensure that laptops, smartphones, tablets, and other computing devices are equipped with security software. Similarly, IoT devices should be appropriately secured based on their specific type. The management of authorized endpoints is typically centralized in businesses, with security systems that communicate with client software on the endpoints. This centralized approach helps enforce policies, detect anomalous activities, prevent data leaks, and thwart attacks.

Creating an inventory of these assets is typically quite straightforward for individuals. Just compile a list of all the devices that you connect to your network. One way to obtain a list is by accessing your router's settings and checking the connected devices section. It is important to remember to include any devices that are only occasionally connected to your network or need to be secured despite not being directly connected to your network. Additionally, please include all storage devices you use, such as external hard drives, flash drives, and memory cards, along with any storage or computing services from third parties, in a separate section. Make sure to write or print the list carefully to avoid any potential problems that may arise from forgetting even a single device.

Ensuring Safety from Potential Hazards

Once you have determined the assets that require protection, it is crucial to establish and enforce the necessary measures to ensure their security and minimize the potential consequences of any potential security breach. When it comes to home users, protection involves setting up barriers to prevent unauthorized access to your digital and physical assets, implementing processes to safeguard your sensitive data (even if they're informal) and regularly creating backups of your configurations and system restore points.

Most individuals have basic elements of protection that they need to consider.

- Perimeter defense
- Firewall/router
- Security software
- Your computer(s) and any other devices you use
- Backup procedures

It is crucial to have a comprehensive understanding of cybersecurity events, including detection, response, device recovery, and defense improvement, to effectively protect against risks.

Perimeter defense

The act of safeguarding your cyber-perimeter can be likened to constructing a moat around a castle, where the goal is to prevent unauthorized access and closely monitor any potential intruders. One way to establish a digital moat is to avoid directly connecting any computer to your Internet modem. It is advisable to connect a firewall/router to the modem and then connect the computers to the firewall/router. The modem can serve as both a firewall and a router, so if your connection is to the firewall/router part rather than the modem itself, that's perfectly fine. Typically, the connection between firewalls and modems is established through a physical network cable. In certain situations, the modem and the firewall/router may be housed in a single physical device.

Firewall/router

The firewall capabilities of modern routers used in home environments are designed to block most forms of inbound traffic unless it is generated as a result of activities initiated by devices protected by the firewall. This means that a firewall can prevent unauthorized access to your computer from external sources, but it won't prevent your computer from receiving responses from a web server if it initiates a request for a web page. Routers employ various technologies to achieve this level of protection. This text highlights the significance of Network Address Translation (NAT), a technology that enables computers on private networks to utilize Internet Protocol (IP) addresses that are not valid for use on the Internet. The Internet perceives all devices on networks using NAT as if they are using a single address. This address belongs to the firewall that acts as an intermediary between these devices and the Internet, managing the NAT function.

Here are some recommendations to enhance the security of your router/firewall:

- Make sure to regularly update your router. It is important to install all updates before using your router for the first time and to regularly check for new updates. If your router has an auto-update feature, be sure to take advantage of that. Your router may have an unpatched vulnerability that could potentially grant unauthorized access to your network.
- Make sure to replace your router once it is no longer supported. If the vendor has ceased support for your router, including updates, it may be a good idea to consider replacing it. Given the lifespan of these devices and networking protocols, there is potential for enhanced performance if you choose to make this change.
- Make sure to update the default administrative password on your firewall/router with a strong and unique password known only to you. Make sure to record both the default and new passwords, and securely store the paper containing them in a safe or safe deposit box. It is not advisable to store passwords on devices that are connected to that network. Make sure to regularly practice logging into the router to avoid forgetting the password.
- Consider choosing a unique name for your Wi-Fi network instead of using the default name provided by your router (also known as its SSID). Suggest a new name.

- Ensure that your Wi-Fi network is configured with encryption, preferably using the WPA2 standard. If available, consider upgrading to the more secure WPA3 standard. These standards are recommended at the time of writing.
- Make sure to set up a password that all devices must know to connect to your Wi-Fi network. Ensure that your password is strong.
- Make sure to disable older Wi-Fi protocols on your router if all your wireless devices are compatible with the modern Wi-Fi 6 and/or Wi-Fi 5 protocols. Disabling protocols like 802.11b, 802.11g, and 802.11n can enhance performance and provide security advantages.
- Make sure to enable MAC address filtering or ensure that everyone in your household is aware that connecting any devices to the wired network requires your permission. In theory, MAC address filtering can effectively restrict network access to only pre-configured devices. It is important to ensure that all devices connected to the network are properly secured before allowing access.
- Make sure to position your wireless router in a central location within your home. By optimizing your signal, you can ensure a stronger connection for yourself while minimizing the chances of others leeching off your network. When setting up a mesh routing system with multiple access points, it is important to carefully follow the instructions provided for locating the devices.
- It is advised not to enable remote access to your router. The desired configuration for the router is to allow management only through connections from protected devices, rather than from external sources. Enabling remote management of a home firewall often poses a significant security risk that outweighs the convenience it offers.
- Make sure to keep an up-to-date record of all the devices that are currently connected to your network. Additionally, please ensure that the list includes devices that are permitted to connect to your network, even if they are not currently connected.
- Ensure network access is provided to desired guests by enabling the guest network feature on the router. Just like the private network, remember to enable encryption and enforce a strong password. Ensure that guests are granted access to the guest network rather than your main network. This also applies to other individuals who require Internet access but may not have your complete trust, such as family members like children.
- If you have a good understanding of technical aspects, consider disabling DHCP and modifying the default IP address range used by the router for the internal network. By doing so, it disrupts certain automated hacking tools and offers additional security advantages. If you're not familiar with such concepts or don't have a clue what the aforementioned sentence means, feel free to disregard this paragraph. Considering the situation, the potential drawbacks of implementing the recommendation may overshadow the security advantages. This is because disabling DHCP and modifying the default IP address range can introduce added technical complications.

Security software

What are the best practices for using security software to safeguard your personal information?

- Ensure that security software is installed on all of your computers and mobile devices. The software should include antivirus and personal device firewall capabilities as essential features.
- Make sure to use anti-spam software on all devices where you access your email.
- Make sure to enable remote wipes on all mobile devices.
- Make sure to set a strong password for logging in to your computer and mobile device.
- Make sure to enable auto-updates whenever possible and always keep your devices updated.

The physical computer(s) and any other endpoints

- For optimal security of your computers and other endpoints, it is crucial to control physical access and store them in a secure location. If someone gains access to a machine in your home, there is a risk of it being stolen, used, or damaged without your knowledge.
- It is advisable to avoid sharing your computer with family members, if possible. For optimal computer sharing, it is recommended to create individual accounts for each family member. Additionally, it is important to avoid granting administrative privileges to other users of the device.
- It is important to not solely depend on deleting data before disposing of, recycling, donating, or selling an old device. Consider using a multi-wipe erasure system for both hard drives and solid-state drives. It is recommended to remove the storage media from the computer before disposing of the device and to physically destroy the storage media.

Additionally, it's important to consider that certain computing devices requiring security may not necessarily be considered "**endpoints**" as they could be connected to other devices. The smart home hub or smart wireless camera system, for example, may have smart devices and/or cameras connected to them using proprietary communication mechanisms. It is crucial to ensure that they are adequately secured.

Backup solutions

Make sure to back up your files regularly. If you are uncertain about the frequency of your backups, likely, that you are not backing up frequently enough.

Detecting

Implementing mechanisms to detect cybersecurity events as quickly as possible after they commence is crucial. Although it may be challenging for home users to afford specialized detection products, it is crucial not to overlook the importance of the detection phase in security. Today, personal computer security software is equipped with a wide range of detection capabilities. It is important to ensure that every device under your management is equipped with security software that actively detects potential intrusions.

Responding

Reacting involves taking action in response to a cybersecurity incident. Security software typically takes action or notifies users when it identifies potential issues.

Recovering

Restoring an impacted computer, network, or device, along with all of its relevant capabilities, to its fully functioning state is the goal of recovery after a cybersecurity event. A formal, written plan for recovery should ideally be documented in advance, ensuring simplicity and clarity in its execution. While it's true that most home users don't typically create one, there are numerous benefits to doing so. Typically, such a plan will be concise, usually less than one page in length.

Assessing Your Existing Security Protocols

Once you have a clear understanding of what you need to safeguard and the necessary measures to do so, it becomes easier to distinguish between your current setup and the ideal protection. Here are some points to keep in mind as you read through the following sections. It's important to note that not all of the following apply in every case:

Software

Consider the following questions for each device when it comes to software and cybersecurity:

- Is all the software packages (including the operating system itself) on your computer obtained legally?
- Were the software packages (including the operating system itself) obtained from trustworthy sources that consistently provide legitimate versions?
- Are all the software packages (including the operating system itself) currently supported by their respective vendors?
- Are all the software packages (including the operating system itself) up-to-date?
- Are all the software packages (including the operating system itself) configured for automatic updates?
- Is there security software installed on the device?
- Does the security software have an auto-update feature enabled?
- Is the security software current?
- Does the security software have anti-malware technology included and is it fully enabled?
- Do virus scans run automatically after every update is applied?
- Does the software have firewall technology and is it fully enabled?
- Does the software have anti-spam technology and is it fully enabled? Is there any other anti-spam software installed and currently running?
- Does the software have the ability to remotely lock or wipe devices, and is this feature fully functional? Is there any other remote lock/remote wipe software installed and currently active?

- Are all the other features of the software enabled? If not, what is it?
- Is there backup software in place to ensure that the device is backed up as part of a comprehensive backup strategy?
- Is encryption enabled for all sensitive data stored on the device?
- Are permissions correctly configured for the software? This ensures that individuals who have access to the device but should not have access to the software are effectively restricted.
- Are the necessary permissions in place to restrict software from making unauthorized changes to the computer (e.g., is any software running with administrator privileges when it shouldn't be)?

These questions pertain to software on a device that is only accessible to trusted users and not exposed to remote outsiders. For devices used in scenarios like a web server, there are additional security concerns that need to be addressed.

Hardware

When it comes to your hardware devices, it's important to ask yourself the following questions:

- Was the hardware acquired from a reliable source? (If you purchased an IP-based camera directly from China through an unfamiliar online retailer, the answer to this question may not be affirmative.)
- How confident are you in your answer to the previous question — and if you have a high level of confidence, what is the basis for your confidence?
- Is the hardware from a brand that the U.S. Government prohibit its agencies due to concerns about security and potential foreign spying or cyber risks?
- Is all of your hardware properly safeguarded against theft and damage, such as rain and electrical spikes, while it is stored in its designated location?
- What safeguards your hardware during its travels?
- Does the device have a backup power source to prevent sudden shutdowns in case of power failure?
- Make sure all your hardware has the latest firmware installed. It's important to download the firmware from a reliable source, like the vendor's website or through the device's configuration tool.
- Is there a BIOS password set on your device, preventing access until the correct password is entered?
- Have you disabled any unnecessary wireless protocols? For enhanced security and improved battery life, it is advisable to disable the Bluetooth radio on your laptop if you are not using it.

Insurance

Although cybersecurity insurance is frequently disregarded, particularly by smaller businesses and individuals, it can effectively help mitigate certain cyber-risks. Considering the specific details of your situation, it may be worth considering the purchase of a policy that protects against specific risks. For small business owners concerned about potential bankruptcy due to a breach, implementing robust security measures is crucial. However, since security measures can never be completely flawless, it might be a prudent decision to invest in a policy that provides coverage for unforeseen catastrophic events. In recent years, cybersecurity policies have become more accessible to individuals and small businesses, expanding beyond the realm of large enterprises.

Learning

Proper education can greatly reduce the risk of individuals in your household (or any other entity) becoming vulnerable to cybersecurity threats.

Here are some points to consider and discuss:

- Are all your family members aware of their rights and responsibilities when it comes to technology in the house, connecting devices to the home network, and allowing guests to connect to the network?
- Have you educated your family members about the potential risks they should be mindful of, such as phishing emails? Are you confident that they understand?
- Have you made sure that all members of your family are aware of cybersecurity best practices, such as avoiding clicking on links in emails?
- Have you made sure that all members of the family are aware of the importance of selecting and protecting passwords for their devices?
- Have you made sure that all family members using social media are aware of the potential risks of oversharing and have a clear understanding of what can and cannot be shared safely?
- Is it clear to everyone in the family the importance of thinking before acting?

Privacy

There are numerous ways in which technology poses a threat to personal privacy: Cameras are constantly monitoring your every move, while technology companies meticulously keep tabs on your online activities through various technical means. Additionally, your mobile devices are constantly keeping track of your whereabouts. Although technology has undoubtedly made it more difficult to maintain privacy compared to a few years ago, privacy is still intact. There are numerous ways to enhance your privacy in today's interconnected world.

Consider the consequences before you decide to share

Many individuals are often quite eager to provide an abundance of information when prompted. Think about the paperwork patients receive at a typical doctor's office in the United States that you have probably been asked to fill out at multiple facilities during your first appointment with the doctor in question. Although some of the answers provided may be useful for the doctor to evaluate and treat you, there are likely other portions that may not be as relevant. Most forms typically require patients to provide their Social Security numbers. This information was necessary many years ago when medical insurance companies frequently used Social Security numbers as insurance ID numbers. However, that risky practice has been discontinued for quite some time now. While it may be true that certain facilities still require your Social Security number for credit reporting purposes, it is important to note that this practice is outdated and potentially unsafe. In most cases, you have the option to leave this field blank. Although it may be hard to imagine that a party collecting your data would misuse it, the more parties that possess your private information and the more extensive and detailed that information becomes, the higher the chances of experiencing a privacy violation as a result of a data breach. When it comes to enhancing your privacy, it's crucial to carefully think about the information you might be sharing about yourself and your loved ones before actually sharing it. It holds in our interactions with government agencies, corporations, medical facilities, and other individuals. It's advisable to refrain from sharing personal information if it's not necessary. Reducing the amount of private information exposed and stored in multiple locations can significantly lower the risk of a privacy breach for individuals.

Consider your words before sharing them online

It is important to carefully consider the potential consequences of sharing any content on social media. Various negative outcomes could arise, such as compromising the privacy of personal information. As an illustration, shared information about a person's family relationships, place of employment, and interests can be exploited by criminals for identity theft and to manipulate their way into your accounts. It is important to be cautious when using your mother's maiden name as a password, whether it is a deliberate choice or a result of a provider's negligence. To prevent criminals from easily discovering this information, avoid listing your mother as your mother on Facebook and refrain from being friends with numerous cousins who share the same last name as your mother's maiden name. It is possible for individuals to easily find out someone's mother's maiden name by looking at their Facebook friends list and identifying the most frequently occurring last name that is different from the account holder's name. This information about a person's children and their schedules can lead to various problems, such as kidnapping, break-ins, or other harmful actions. It is important to be cautious when sharing such details.

It is important to be cautious when sharing information related to medical activities, as it could potentially result in the disclosure of sensitive and private information. As an illustration, photographs or location data that show a person at a specific medical facility could reveal that the person has a condition that the facility is renowned for treating. Sharing different types of information or images can have consequences for a user's relationships and result in the disclosure of private information. The act of sharing information or images can inadvertently expose private details about someone's involvement in potentially sensitive activities. These activities may include consuming alcohol or using recreational drugs, handling weapons, affiliating with controversial organizations, and more. Revealing one's presence at a specific place and time can unintentionally jeopardize the confidentiality of sensitive information. Additionally, it's important to note that the issue of oversharing extends beyond just social networks. Sharing excessive amounts of information through various digital platforms has become a significant issue in today's society. Occasionally, individuals may not be aware of their tendency to overshare, leading to the inadvertent inclusion of incorrect data in emails or attachments of wrong files.

Tips for maintaining your privacy

Aside from being mindful of what you share, there are a few other steps you can take to minimize the potential risks of oversharing:

- Ensure you use the privacy settings on your social media accounts. It is important to be cautious about sharing personal information (as discussed earlier). Ensure that your privacy settings on social media are configured to safeguard your data from being seen by the general public unless the specific post is meant for public consumption. However, it is not advisable to depend solely on them. Do not solely depend on social media security settings for safeguarding the privacy of your information. Repetitive discoveries have revealed significant vulnerabilities that undermine the effectiveness of security controls on various platforms.
- It is advisable to refrain from storing sensitive information in the cloud unless proper encryption measures are taken. It is important to ensure that private information is properly encrypted before storing it in the cloud. It is important to not solely depend on the encryption offered by the cloud provider for safeguarding your privacy. In certain situations, the encryption can also be compromised if the provider is breached. If you need to store sensitive information in the cloud, it is important to encrypt it yourself before uploading it, regardless of the encryption used by the cloud provider. Applications exist that can streamline this process for popular cloud storage providers. These applications can automatically encrypt and upload any files placed in a designated folder on your computer.
- Avoid storing sensitive information in cloud applications that are primarily intended for sharing and collaboration. It is advisable not to store sensitive information such as passwords, identification documents, or confidential medical records in a Google doc. Although it may appear obvious, numerous individuals still engage in this behavior.
- Make use of the privacy settings in your browser or consider using Tor for enhanced privacy. If you're concerned about accessing material without leaving a trace, there are a few steps you can take. First, consider using Private/Incognito Mode in your web browser, although it's important to note that this only provides limited protection. Alternatively, if it's an option for you, you might want to consider using a web browser like the Tor Browser Bundle. This browser offers obfuscated routing, default strong privacy settings, and various preconfigured privacy add-ons to enhance your privacy.
- It's important to be cautious when using a browser to avoid being tracked. When you search for detailed information on a medical condition in a normal browser window, different parties will likely take advantage of that data. You may have noticed the impact of this tracking, such as when advertisements on one webpage are relevant to something you previously searched for on another.

- Keep your real cellphone number private. Consider obtaining a forwarding number from a reliable service such as Google Voice. It is advisable to provide this number instead of your personal cell phone number. By taking this precaution, you can effectively safeguard yourself against various risks such as SIM swapping and spam.
- Make sure to keep your private content stored offline. For optimal security, it is recommended to keep extremely sensitive materials offline, either in a fireproof safe or a bank-safe deposit box. If you prefer to store them electronically, it is advisable to keep them on a computer that is not connected to any network.
- Ensure that all private information, including documents, images, videos, and more, is encrypted for added security. When it comes to encryption, it's better to err on the side of caution.
- When using online chat, it is advisable to use end-to-end encryption. It's important to be aware that any text messages sent through regular cell phone service (SMS messages) have the potential to be read by unauthorized individuals. It is advisable to refrain from sharing sensitive information in written form. When it comes to sharing sensitive information in writing, it is important to encrypt the data.

A chat application that offers end-to-end encryption is the simplest method for encrypting data. This encryption method ensures that your messages are secure and cannot be easily accessed by hackers. Messages are encrypted on your device and decrypted on the recipient's device, making it difficult for anyone to intercept and read them. By utilizing end-to-end encryption, the provider's servers become a more challenging target for hackers attempting to breach and access your messages. (Occasionally, providers falsely assert that hackers are unable to read such messages at all, which is inaccurate. There are two reasons for this: 1. It is possible for hackers to access the metadata, such as your chat history and timestamps. 2. If hackers successfully infiltrate internal servers, they could potentially upload a compromised version of the app to the app store, which may include a hidden backdoor. WhatsApp is widely recognized as the leading chat application that implements end-to-end encryption.

- Remember to practice proper cyber-hygiene. Practicing proper cyber-hygiene is crucial for maintaining privacy, especially considering the amount of sensitive information stored electronically.

Ensuring Secure Online Banking

In today's modern age, it is not practical for most people to avoid online banking due to the security concerns it raises. Additionally, there are other potential risks associated with both phone-based banking and in-person banking. Thankfully, you can still enjoy the conveniences of online banking while ensuring your security. I have a deep understanding of the risks associated with online banking, as I have been using it since it was introduced by major financial institutions in the mid-1990s as a replacement for direct-dial-up banking services.

Here are some recommendations to enhance your online banking security:

- Make sure your online banking password is strong, unique, and something you can easily remember. Storing it in a database, password manager, or any other electronic location is not recommended. (Keeping a physical copy in a safe deposit box, while not often required, can be a viable option if you prefer to have a hard copy.)
- Select a random Personal Identification Number (PIN) for your ATM card and/or phone identification. For banking-related purposes, it is important to use a PIN that is completely unrelated to any information that you are familiar with. It is important to avoid using a PIN that has been used for any other purpose. Additionally, it is crucial not to create PINs or passwords that are based on the one chosen for your ATM card. It is important to never write down your PIN. Do not include it in any computer file. It is important to never disclose your PIN to anyone, even if they are bank employees.
- You may want to consider requesting an ATM card from your bank that is solely for ATM use and cannot be used as a debit card. Although these cards do not have the functionality to make purchases, if you prefer using credit cards for your purchases, the lack of a purchase feature on your ATM card is not a concern. Preventing the card from being used as a debit card increases the likelihood that only someone who knows your PIN can withdraw money from your account. Another crucial aspect is that malfunctioning ATM cards cannot be utilized by criminals to make unauthorized transactions.
- If your debit card is used fraudulently, you may find yourself in a situation where you have lost money and need to take steps to recover it. In the unfortunate event of fraudulent credit card usage, you will not be held responsible for any financial losses, unless a thorough investigation proves otherwise.
- Make sure to log in to online banking from devices that you trust and have proper security measures in place. It's important to keep your devices up to date with the latest security software.
- Make sure to only log in to online banking from secure networks that you trust. When traveling, it is advisable to rely on your cellular provider's connection instead of using public Wi-Fi. Avoid logging into online banking or any other sensitive apps from locations where communication providers are suspected of targeting malware devices connecting to their networks.
- Access your online banking by logging in through a web browser or the official app provided by the bank. It is important to always log in from the official app store for your device's platform and avoid using third-party apps.
- Consider signing up for alerts from your bank. It would be beneficial to set up notifications via text message and/or email for any new payee additions, withdrawals, and other relevant activities.
- Make sure to enable multi factor authentication and take steps to secure any device used for this purpose. In the unfortunate event that your phone, which is used for generating one-time passwords, gets stolen, the thief gains temporary access to your second factor, leaving you unable to use it.

- Make sure to avoid storing your online banking password in your browser. It is important to avoid writing down your online banking password, especially in a system that automatically enters it for you when using a web browser.
- Remember to always enter the URL of your bank whenever you visit their website. Avoid clicking on any links to it.
- It is recommended to use a different computer for online banking than the one you use for online shopping, email access, and social media. If it's not feasible or convenient, consider using an alternative web browser and make sure to regularly update it.
- For added security, consider setting up your browser to remember an incorrect password for a website. This way, if someone gains access to your device, they will have a harder time logging into that site with your credentials.
- It is important to ensure the security of all devices used for online banking. It is important to take proper precautions when it comes to securing your devices. This includes physically keeping them safe, such as not leaving them unattended on a table in a restaurant while using the restroom. Additionally, it is crucial to set up a password to unlock your devices and consider enabling remote wipes as an added layer of security.
- Make sure to keep an eye on your account for any suspicious activity.

Using Smart Devices with Safety in Mind

Smart devices and the so-called Internet of Things pose a variety of cybersecurity risks. Here are some suggestions on how to enhance your security while using such devices:

- Ensure that all of your IoT devices do not pose any security risks in the event of a failure. It is crucial to avoid any scenario where a smart lock hinders your ability to exit a room in the event of a fire or allows intruders to enter your home during a power outage or network failure.
- Consider running your IoT devices on a separate network from your computers, if possible. It is essential to have a firewall protecting the IoT network.
- Ensure that all IoT devices are regularly updated. IoT devices have been targeted by hackers who have taken advantage of vulnerabilities, allowing them to seize control of the devices and orchestrate significant attacks. It is advisable to enable the firmware auto-update capability if available on the device.
- Make sure to maintain an up-to-date record of all the devices that are currently connected to your network. Additionally, it is important to maintain a record of all devices that are authorized to connect, even if they are not currently connected.
- Remember to disconnect devices when they're not in use, if possible. When a device is offline, it becomes inaccessible to anyone who is not physically present at the device, making it secure from hacking attempts.
- Ensure that all devices are password-protected. It is important to avoid using the default passwords that come with devices. Every device needs to have its login and password.
- Make sure to review the settings on your devices. Default setting values on many devices are often lacking in terms of security.

- Ensure the security of your smartphone, both physically and digitally. It probably operates applications that have access to some or all of your devices.
- Consider disabling unnecessary device features, if possible. This action effectively minimizes the attack surface, decreasing the opportunities for unauthorized users to attempt hacking into the device. Additionally, it significantly reduces the likelihood of the device being vulnerable to exploitable software weaknesses.

The convenience of Universal Plug and Play (UPnP) in simplifying device setup comes with certain risks. Hackers can easily discover and target devices due to vulnerabilities in many UPnP implementations. Additionally, UPnP can potentially enable malware to bypass firewall security measures and allow hackers to execute commands on routers.

Frequently Asked Questions

1. How do you ensure safety from potential hazards?
2. How do you access your existing security protocols?
3. What are the tips for maintaining your privacy?
4. How do you ensure secure online banking?
5. How do you understand endpoints?

CHAPTER FIVE
INTRODUCTION TO ENCRYPTION

Overview

Chapter five focuses on encryption as an important discussion in cybersecurity. Here, you will learn about encryption and how it is used in cybersecurity.

About Encryption

In today's fast-paced digital era, where information travels rapidly through expansive networks, the significance of safeguarding sensitive data cannot be emphasized enough. Cybersecurity has emerged as a crucial concern for individuals, businesses, and governments alike. Encryption is a highly effective and essential tool in the world of data security, offering a wide range of techniques to protect valuable information.

The process of encryption ensures that only authorized parties can access encoded information. The process includes transforming plain text or data into an unreadable format, referred to as ciphertext, through the use of cryptographic algorithms. Those who possess the appropriate decryption key can decrypt the ciphertext back into its original form. The process ensures a high level of security to safeguard data from any unauthorized access or interception. The history of encryption stretches back for thousands of years, as ancient civilizations used basic methods to hide messages from unwanted eyes. Although the development of encryption took time, it reached a new level of complexity with the introduction of modern cryptography in the 20th century. Today, encryption is an essential component of cybersecurity, ensuring the security of communication channels and safeguarding stored data. Encryption plays a crucial role in safeguarding the privacy of sensitive data. Encrypting data before transmission or storage helps organizations safeguard against unauthorized access or tampering. In industries like finance, healthcare, and government, the protection of sensitive data is of utmost importance due to the potentially severe consequences of its loss or compromise. Encryption plays a crucial role in authentication and identity verification. The use of digital signatures, which rely on cryptographic algorithms, enables individuals and organizations to easily verify the authenticity and integrity of electronic documents or messages. This effectively addresses fraud and guarantees the authenticity and reliability of communications. Encryption is crucial for ensuring the security and reliability of data. Encrypting information at rest helps organizations prevent unauthorized modifications or tampering. It is crucial to prioritize data integrity in environments where it is of utmost importance, such as critical infrastructure systems or electronic voting systems. In addition, encryption allows for secure communication over public networks, like the internet. Through the use of protocols like SSL/TLS (Secure Sockets Layer/Transport Layer Security), organizations can guarantee the confidentiality of sensitive information while it is being transmitted. Privacy and security are of utmost importance in activities such as online banking, e-commerce, and remote work. Furthermore, encryption is essential for ensuring regulatory compliance, in addition to its practical applications. Numerous industries must adhere to strict data protection regulations, including the Health Insurance Portability and Accountability Act (HIPAA) in healthcare and the General Data Protection Regulation (GDPR) in the European Union. Encryption plays a crucial role in compliance efforts, enabling organizations to fulfill the requirements of safeguarding sensitive data and upholding privacy rights.

While encryption offers many advantages, it is important to acknowledge the hurdles and constraints it presents. One of the main obstacles is finding the right balance between security and usability. Although encryption offers strong protection against unauthorized access, it can also bring about complexity and inconvenience for end-users. Organizations must take into account various factors when implementing encryption solutions, such as managing encryption keys, ensuring system compatibility, and addressing performance concerns. It's important to note that encryption alone cannot eliminate cybersecurity threats. Although it can help reduce various risks, it cannot eliminate them. Even with encryption in place, sophisticated adversaries can still find ways to bypass it. They may use techniques like social engineering, malware, or exploiting vulnerabilities in cryptographic algorithms. Furthermore, the rapid advancement of quantum computing raises concerns about the vulnerability of current encryption standards. Theoretically, quantum computers have the potential to compromise numerous widely employed encryption algorithms. Despite the difficulties, encryption continues to be a fundamental aspect of contemporary cybersecurity practices. Technology is constantly advancing, leading to ongoing improvements in encryption techniques. Researchers and practitioners are dedicated to creating stronger and more reliable solutions. Understanding the principles and applications of encryption is crucial for organizations to safeguard their data and maintain the trust of their stakeholders in today's interconnected world.

Encryption Basics

In today's interconnected digital world, where data is crucial for businesses and individuals, safeguarding sensitive information from unauthorized access is of utmost importance. Encryption is a crucial component of cybersecurity, offering protection against malicious individuals and guaranteeing the privacy, accuracy, and legitimacy of information. This guide provides a thorough exploration of encryption, covering its principles, methodologies, and applications in protecting digital assets.

What exactly is encryption?

The essence of encryption lies in transforming plain, readable data, also known as plaintext, into an incomprehensible form called ciphertext, through the use of an algorithm and a cryptographic key. The transformation ensures that the original data remains secure and inaccessible to unauthorized individuals, as it can only be deciphered with the appropriate decryption key. Encryption is an incredibly effective tool for safeguarding a wide range of sensitive information, including personal communications, financial transactions, government secrets, and intellectual property.

Exploring the Fundamentals of Encryption

Encryption is dependent on two main components: algorithms and keys.

1. **Algorithms**: The topic of algorithms revolves around encryption algorithms, which are mathematical procedures specifically created to manipulate data in a manner that renders it incomprehensible to anyone without authorized access. The complexity of these algorithms varies, with some using symmetric encryption, where a single key is used for both encryption and decryption, while others use asymmetric encryption, where different keys are used for encryption and decryption.
2. **Keys**: Encryption keys are strings of data that play a crucial role in controlling the encryption and decryption processes. The concept of symmetric encryption involves the use of a single key that is shared between the sender and the recipient. On the other hand, asymmetric encryption utilizes two keys: a public key, which is widely distributed and used for encryption, and a private key, which is kept secret and used for decryption. The effectiveness of encryption is heavily influenced by the length and randomness of the keys used.

Various Encryption Methods

There are two main categories of encryption techniques: symmetric encryption and asymmetric encryption.

1. **Symmetric Encryption**: Secret-key encryption, also referred to as symmetric encryption, uses a single key for both the encryption and decryption procedures. The efficiency of this

encryption method is enhanced by its simplicity, allowing for the encryption of large volumes of data. Some commonly used symmetric encryption algorithms are Advanced Encryption Standard (AES), Data Encryption Standard (DES), and Triple DES.

2. **Asymmetric Encryption**: In the world of encryption, there exists a method known as asymmetric encryption or public-key encryption. This method involves the use of two keys: a public key, which is widely shared and employed for encryption purposes, and a private key, which is kept confidential and used for decryption. This method allows for secure communication between parties without the requirement of exchanging secret keys in advance. Some widely used asymmetric encryption algorithms are RSA (Rivest-Shamir-Adleman) and Elliptic Curve Cryptography (ECC).

Uses of Encryption

Encryption is crucial in multiple areas of cybersecurity and beyond:

1. **Communication Security:** Encryption guarantees the privacy of important data sent over networks, including emails, instant messages, and voice calls. Communication protocols like HTTPS (Hypertext Transfer Protocol Secure) use encryption to safeguard data transmitted between web browsers and servers.

2. **Data Storage**: Encryption provides a secure layer of protection for data stored on various devices, including computers, smartphones, and servers. Disk encryption solutions provide a high level of security by encrypting entire disk volumes, ensuring that stored data remains protected even in the event of physical storage compromise.

3. **Authentication**: Encryption plays a crucial role in digital signatures and certificate-based authentication, ensuring the legitimacy and security of digital documents and communications. The use of digital signatures allows for the verification of the sender's identity and ensures the integrity of the message or document.

4. **Ensuring Secure Transactions:** Online transactions, such as e-commerce purchases, online banking, and electronic funds transfers, are safeguarded through encryption. The transmission of payment card data, personal information, and transaction details is encrypted to minimize the risk of interception or fraud.

5. **VPN**: Virtual Private Networks (VPNs) use encryption to establish secure, encrypted tunnels between users and remote servers, safeguarding data traffic from unauthorized access and interception. Users can enjoy enhanced privacy and anonymity when accessing the internet from networks that may be less secure, such as public Wi-Fi hotspots.

Challenges and Considerations

Although encryption is a powerful tool for safeguarding sensitive information, it does come with its fair share of challenges and considerations:

1. **Key Management**: Encryption is only as strong as the practices used to generate, distribute, and store encryption keys. It is crucial to have robust key management

practices in place to ensure security. Properly managing keys is crucial to maintaining the security of encrypted data.

2. **Performance Overhead**: The computational overhead caused by encryption and decryption processes can harm system performance, especially in resource-constrained environments like embedded systems or mobile devices. It is crucial to strike a balance between security requirements and performance considerations.

3. **Cryptographic Vulnerabilities:** There is a possibility that cryptographic algorithms and implementations may have vulnerabilities that attackers could exploit to bypass encryption or recover plaintext data. Regular cryptographic reviews and updates are essential to address these risks effectively.

4. **Compliance with Regulations**: Organizations must adhere to regulatory requirements regarding encryption, especially in industries that handle sensitive data like healthcare, finance, and government. Adhering to standards like the General Data Protection Regulation (GDPR) or the Health Insurance Portability and Accountability Act (HIPAA) is crucial.

5. **Emerging Technologies:** The rise of quantum computing brings about a possible challenge to conventional encryption algorithms, as these powerful machines have the potential to crack specific cryptographic schemes. Ongoing research is being conducted to address the challenge of quantum-resistant algorithms and post-quantum cryptography.

An Overview of Encryption Algorithms

The process of encryption involves encoding information in a manner that restricts access to only those who are authorized. The process uses algorithms and keys to convert plain text into ciphertext, rendering it unintelligible to any unauthorized individuals who may intercept it. The process of decryption involves converting ciphertext back into its original form.

Various Encryption Algorithms

There are two main categories of encryption algorithms: symmetric and asymmetric encryption.

1. **Symmetric Encryption**: Symmetric encryption, also referred to as secret-key encryption, uses a single key for both the encryption and decryption processes. It is crucial to maintain the security of the shared key, as it is used by both the sender and the recipient. Some of the widely used symmetric encryption algorithms are:

- **Advanced Encryption Standard (AES):** AES is a highly popular symmetric encryption algorithm that is widely used. The system provides excellent security and efficiency and is widely used in a range of applications, such as safeguarding data during transmission and protecting stored information.

- **Data Encryption Standard:** DES, being one of the earliest encryption standards, has been largely replaced by AES due to its vulnerability to brute-force attacks.

- **Triple DES:** The Triple DES (3DES) algorithm applies the DES algorithm three times to each data block, significantly enhancing its security.
2. **Asymmetric Encryption:** Public-key encryption, also referred to as asymmetric encryption, involves the use of a public key and a private key. The public key is widely distributed and serves the purpose of encryption, while the private key remains confidential and is used for decryption. Although asymmetric encryption provides enhanced security, it does require more computational resources. Some commonly used asymmetric encryption algorithms are:
- **Rivest-Shami-Adleman:** RSA is considered one of the earliest and most widely used asymmetric encryption algorithms. The security of this system is based on the challenge of factoring large prime numbers.
- **Elliptic Curve Cryptography:** ECC is becoming increasingly popular because of its efficiency and smaller key sizes compared to RSA. This makes it a great choice for resource-constrained environments like mobile devices and IoT devices.

Advantages and Disadvantages

Every encryption algorithm has its own set of strengths and weaknesses that dictate its appropriateness for different applications.

- **Symmetric Encryption**: Symmetric encryption algorithms are known for their speed and efficiency, making them a great choice for encrypting large amounts of data. Although the distribution of the secret key remains a challenge, it is crucial for secure communication between the parties involved.
- **Asymmetric Encryption**: Public and private key pairs are used in asymmetric encryption to address the key distribution problem. The system provides enhanced security and enables secure communication without the need for pre-established key exchange. On the other hand, asymmetric encryption requires more computational power and may not be the best choice for encrypting large volumes of data.

Applications in Cybersecurity

Encryption algorithms are extensively used in a range of cybersecurity applications to ensure the confidentiality, integrity, and authenticity of data.

1. **Communication Security**: Encryption guarantees the confidentiality and security of data exchanged between parties during transmission. The use of encryption algorithms in secure protocols like SSL/TLS ensures that sensitive information, such as financial transactions, personal messages, and login credentials, is protected when establishing secure connections over the internet.
2. **Data Storage:** Encryption is used to safeguard data stored on various devices, including computers, smartphones, and servers. The entire storage volume is encrypted with full disk encryption, ensuring that data remains secure even in the event of theft or loss. File-

level encryption provides users with the ability to encrypt individual files or folders, enhancing the overall security of their data.

3. **Digital Signatures**: Asymmetric encryption algorithms are used in digital signatures to ensure the authenticity and integrity of digital documents and messages. The process of digital signatures involves the utilization of the sender's private key to encrypt a hash of the message. This encrypted hash can then be decrypted using the sender's public key to verify the authenticity of the signature.

4. **Ensuring Password Protection**: Encryption algorithms are utilized to securely store and transmit passwords and other sensitive authentication credentials. The process of hashing passwords involves using one-way hash functions, which makes it extremely difficult to reverse the process and retrieve the original password.

Public Key Infrastructure (PKI)

PKI is essential for maintaining cybersecurity, as it provides the foundation for secure communication and authentication in digital environments. Let's explore the intricacies of PKI, diving into its components, functions, and the crucial role it plays in protecting sensitive information in the digital world. The foundation of PKI is a comprehensive system that encompasses policies, procedures, technology, and personnel to effectively manage digital certificates and public-key encryption. The main objective is to enable secure communication over networks that are not secure, such as the internet.

PKI Components

They include the following:

1. **Certificate Authority**: The Certificate Authority is a reliable entity that is responsible for issuing digital certificates. This statement highlights the importance of certificates in establishing the identity of individuals or entities by linking a public key to them. CAs are crucial for establishing trust within a PKI framework.

2. **The Registration Authority (RA):** RA serves as a bridge between users and the CA. The main purpose of this is to authenticate the identities of individuals or entities who are applying for digital certificates, before sending the request to the CA for approval.

3. **Public Key Cryptography**: Asymmetric cryptography is the foundation of PKI, utilizing public and private key pairs. The distribution of public keys is extensive, as they are used for data encryption. Conversely, private keys are strictly safeguarded and used for decryption purposes. The cryptographic mechanism guarantees a high level of security in communication between parties.

4. **Digital Certificates**: PKI relies heavily on digital certificates. The documents provide details about the entity they are issued to, such as their public key and identity information. The authenticity of these certificates is ensured through digital signatures by the CA.

5. **Revoking Certificates**: Revoking digital certificates is crucial to prevent unauthorized access in case of compromise or expiration. PKI incorporates mechanisms for certificate revocation and the management of current Certificate Revocation Lists (CRLs) or the use of the Online Certificate Status Protocol (OCSP) for instantaneous validation.

PKI functions

1. **Verification**: PKI facilitates secure authentication by enabling parties to verify each other's identities through digital certificates. Only authorized users can access sensitive information or services, ensuring security.
2. **Encryption**: It explains how PKI enabled secure communication through the use of public and private keys. It highlights the importance of encryption in protecting data. The data transmission process guarantees confidentiality and integrity.
3. **Digital Signatures:** The use of private keys to generate digital signatures ensures that the sender cannot deny sending a message, providing a strong level of non-repudiation. PKI allows for the validation of digital signatures through the use of public keys, ensuring trust and accountability.
4. **Secure Transactions:** PKI plays a crucial role in ensuring the security of online transactions, including e-commerce and online banking. Through the implementation of encryption and authentication measures, PKI effectively reduces the likelihood of fraudulent activities and unauthorized entry.
5. **Access Control Security:** Implementing PKI enables organizations to establish strong access control measures by verifying the identity of users and devices before granting them access to sensitive resources. This feature ensures that only authorized individuals can access the system and provides protection against potential threats from within the organization.

The Significance of PKI in Cybersecurity

1. **Building Confidence**: The trust in digital transactions is established by PKI through the verification of the identities of all parties involved and the assurance of data integrity and authenticity. It is essential to uphold trust in online interactions.
2. **Maintaining Confidentiality**: Through the use of public key cryptography, PKI ensures the protection of sensitive information when it is transmitted over networks that are not secure. This is crucial for safeguarding sensitive data from prying eyes and malicious individuals.
3. **Ensuring Regulatory Compliance:** PKI has a crucial role in ensuring regulatory compliance, especially in industries like healthcare, finance, and government. These sectors have strict standards for data privacy and security. Implementing PKI is crucial for organizations to meet regulatory requirements and avoid potential fines or penalties.
4. **Addressing Potential Risks:** PKI is effective in reducing a range of cybersecurity risks, such as data breaches, identity theft, and man-in-the-middle attacks. With its robust authentication and encryption mechanisms, PKI significantly enhances the security of organizations and minimizes their vulnerability to cyber threats.

5. **Embracing the Era of Digital Transformation**: PKI plays a crucial role in today's digital landscape, ensuring secure communication and transactions across a wide range of platforms and devices. This text highlights the importance of secure connectivity in various technological areas such as IoT devices, cloud computing, and mobile applications. It emphasizes how this connectivity enables smooth digital transformation efforts.

Challenges and Considerations

While PKI implementation offers many advantages, it is important to be aware of the challenges and considerations that come with it. Here are some examples:

1. **Complexity of Management**: Managing a PKI infrastructure can be a complex and resource-intensive task. It requires dedicated personnel and robust processes to handle certificate issuance, renewal, and revocation effectively.
2. **Managing Keys:** Effective key management is essential for maintaining the security and integrity of PKI. Organizations must ensure the secure storage and protection of private keys to prevent any unauthorized access or misuse.
3. **Scalability**: As organizations continue to grow and expand their digital presence, the ability to scale becomes a crucial factor to consider when implementing PKI. The infrastructure needs to be able to efficiently handle the growing demands of certificate issuance and management.
4. **Interoperability**: It is crucial to have seamless integration and operation by ensuring interoperability between different PKI components and systems. Standards like X.509 can enhance interoperability, although they may necessitate meticulous configuration and management.
5. **Compliance Requirements**: Implementing PKI becomes more complex when considering the need to meet regulatory compliance requirements, such as GDPR, HIPAA, or PCI DSS. Organizations must ensure that their PKI practices are in line with the applicable regulations and standards to avoid any potential non-compliance issues.

Anticipated Developments in PKI

In PKI and cybersecurity, several trends are significantly influencing the future:

1. **Exploring Quantum-Safe Cryptography**: There is a rising concern regarding the vulnerability of existing cryptographic algorithms due to the emergence of quantum computing. PKI will probably adapt to include quantum-safe cryptography, which will provide robust protection against quantum attacks.

2. **Streamlining Processes:** The role of automation and orchestration technologies in PKI management is becoming increasingly significant. These technologies streamline processes, minimize human error, and improve operational efficiency.

3. **Decentralized Identity:** The idea of decentralized identity, made possible by technologies like blockchain, has the potential to revolutionize PKI. It empowers individuals to have more control over their digital identities and reduces the need for centralized authorities.
4. **Security with Zero Trust**: The adoption of Zero Trust Security principles will have a significant impact on PKI architectures, resulting in stronger authentication and access control mechanisms.
5. **Cloud-Based PKI Solutions**: Cloud-based PKI solutions are becoming increasingly popular due to their scalability, flexibility, and cost-effectiveness when compared to traditional on-premises deployments. Cloud-based PKI is expected to become more common as organizations adopt cloud technologies.

Encrypting Data at Rest and in Transit

Data at rest is data that is stored on physical or digital media, like hard drives, databases, or cloud storage and is not currently being transferred between systems. The process of securing data at rest entails encrypting it in a manner that renders it indecipherable to unauthorized individuals, even if they manage to gain access to the storage medium without the encryption key.

Methods for Securing Data in Storage

1. **Full Disk Encryption:** FDE provides a high level of security by encrypting the entire storage device, and safeguarding all the data stored on it. This approach is especially beneficial for devices such as laptops and mobile phones, given the increased likelihood of physical theft.
2. **File-level Encryption**: In contrast to FDE, which encrypts the entire disk, file-level encryption offers the flexibility to selectively encrypt specific files or folders. This feature provides a higher level of control over the encryption of data, which can be beneficial in situations where certain files contain sensitive information.
3. **Database Encryption**: Databases are highly sought after by attackers due to the valuable information they contain. Adding encryption to data within databases enhances security measures, effectively safeguarding sensitive records from unauthorized access.

Encrypting Data in Transit

Data in transit refers to the movement of data between systems, like when you send an email or browse the web. Ensuring data is encrypted during transit provides an additional layer of security, making it extremely difficult for unauthorized individuals to understand the information being transmitted.

Methods for Securing Data during Transmission

1. **Transport Layer Security**: TLS, the successor to SSL, is the most widely used protocol for encrypting data in transit on the internet. It is highly regarded for its effectiveness in

securing data. The secure connection between client and server is established using a combination of symmetric and asymmetric encryption.

2. **Secure Shell**: SSH is a network protocol that ensures secure communication over an unsecured network through encryption. It is frequently utilized for remote login and command execution, as well as for secure file transfer (SFTP).

3. **Virtual Private Networks (VPNs)** establish a secure and encrypted connection between a user's device and a remote server, ensuring that their online activities remain private and protected from unauthorized access. They are frequently utilized to enhance privacy and security while connecting to public Wi-Fi networks or circumventing geo-restrictions.

Challenges and Considerations

Encryption is a powerful tool for safeguarding data, but it comes with its fair share of obstacles and factors to consider.

1. **Key Management:** Effective key management is crucial for maintaining the security of encryption. It is crucial to maintain the integrity of encrypted data by following proper key management practices, which include key generation, storage, rotation, and revocation.

2. **Performance Impact:** The process of encrypting and decrypting data can introduce overhead, potentially affecting system performance, especially in high-throughput environments. Ensuring optimal system performance requires careful consideration of both security requirements and performance considerations.

3. **Compliance and Regulation**: Organizations in regulated industries must adhere to data protection regulations and standards like GDPR, HIPAA, and PCI DSS. Implementing encryption measures alongside compliance necessitates meticulous planning and execution.

4. **User Experience**: Encryption should not overly inconvenience end-users or hinder their ability to access and use data. Ensuring a smooth user experience requires finding the right balance between security requirements and usability considerations.

Using Secure Communication Protocols

Communication protocols are essential for establishing secure channels of communication in different digital environments. The data transmitted between two or more entities is kept confidential, tamper-proof, and authenticated. The protocols employ cryptographic techniques to secure data, verify users or systems, and thwart unauthorized access or interception by malicious actors.

The main goals of secure communication protocols are:

1. **Privacy**: Guarantee that the information shared between parties is kept confidential and inaccessible to unauthorized individuals.

2. **Integrity**: Ensuring the integrity of data is of utmost importance, as it safeguards against any unauthorized tampering or modification during transmission.
3. **Authentication**: This is the process of verifying the identities of communicating parties to establish trust and prevent impersonation or spoofing attacks.
4. **Non-repudiation**: Establishing accountability and trust by ensuring that the sender of a message cannot deny sending it, and the recipient cannot deny receiving it, is a crucial aspect of non-repudiation.

Secure Communication Protocols Types

Communication protocols play a crucial role in ensuring the security of various applications and environments by using a wide array of technologies and standards.

Here are a few protocols that are frequently used:

1. **Transport Layer Security (TLS)/Secure Sockets Layer (SSL):** TLS and its predecessor SSL are cryptographic protocols that ensure secure communication over a network. They are commonly used in web browsing, email, instant messaging, and other applications that necessitate secure data transmission. The TLS/SSL protocols provide a secure way to encrypt data exchanged between the client and server, guaranteeing both confidentiality and integrity.
2. **Internet Protocol Security (IPsec):** IPsec is a suite of protocols that ensures the security of Internet Protocol (IP) communications. It achieves this by authenticating and encrypting each IP packet of a communication session. This operates at the network layer of the OSI model and is frequently used in virtual private networks (VPNs) to create secure connections between remote sites or devices.
3. **Secure Shell (SSH):** SSH is a cryptographic network protocol that enables secure remote access to a computer or server over an unsecured network. This software offers robust encryption and authentication features, making it highly desirable for ensuring security in command-line operations, file transfers, and tunneling applications.
4. **Pretty Good Privacy (PGP)/OpenPGP:** PGP, also known as Pretty Good Privacy, is a powerful program designed to ensure the utmost privacy and authentication for data communication through encryption and decryption techniques. OpenPGP is a fantastic open-source implementation of the PGP standard that allows for secure email communication, file encryption, and digital signatures.
5. **Wireless Security Protocols (WPA2, WPA3):** WPA2 (Wi-Fi Protected Access 2) and its successor WPA3 are security protocols that aim to enhance the security of wireless networks. The data transmitted over Wi-Fi networks is protected from eavesdropping and unauthorized access through the use of encryption techniques like Advanced Encryption Standard (AES).

The Importance of Secure Communication Protocols in Cybersecurity

Communication protocols that prioritize security are crucial for bolstering cybersecurity for both organizations and individuals. **They effectively address a wide range of cyber threats and vulnerabilities. Here are some important aspects of their role:**

1. Secure communication protocols use robust encryption techniques to ensure that data transmissions remain secure and impervious to interception. This safeguards sensitive information from falling into the wrong hands. This ensures the protection of sensitive information, including personal credentials, financial transactions, and proprietary business data, from unauthorized access.

2. The prevention of Man-in-the-Middle Attacks involves the use of cryptographic techniques like digital certificates and key exchanges. These secure communication protocols ensure that the identities of the communicating parties are verified and any attempts by malicious intermediaries to intercept or manipulate data are detected. This effectively prevents man-in-the-middle attacks, where malicious individuals intercept communication between two parties to steal sensitive information or impersonate one of the parties.

3. In a remote work environment, it is crucial to have secure communication protocols like SSL VPNs and SSH to ensure safe remote access to corporate networks and resources. Through the implementation of robust encryption and stringent authentication measures, these protocols guarantee the secure access of sensitive data and systems by remote employees, regardless of their location, without any compromise to security.

4. TLS/SSL protocols play a crucial role in ensuring the safety of various online transactions, including e-commerce purchases, online banking, and electronic payments. This protocol ensures the security of sensitive financial data, such as credit card numbers and personal information, by encrypting it. As a result, it effectively safeguards against fraud, identity theft, and unauthorized access to payment information.

5. Communication protocols that prioritize security allow for safe collaboration and sharing of information between individuals and organizations, even when they are located far apart. From exchanging confidential documents via encrypted email to conducting secure video conferences over VPNs, these protocols guarantee the protection of sensitive information from unauthorized access or interception.

Challenges and Considerations

Secure communication protocols encounter various challenges and considerations that must be addressed to ensure robust cybersecurity.

1. Cyber threats are constantly evolving, with attackers using sophisticated techniques to exploit vulnerabilities in communication protocols and systems. To stay ahead of these threats, it is crucial to prioritize continuous monitoring, threat intelligence, and proactive security measures.

2. Ensuring compatibility and interoperability between different secure communication protocols and systems can be quite challenging, especially in environments with diverse technologies and standards. It is crucial for organizations to thoroughly assess and adopt protocols that can seamlessly integrate with their current infrastructure and applications.
3. The performance and overhead of encryption and decryption processes in secure communication protocols can have an impact on system performance, especially in high-volume network environments. Ensuring optimal network performance while maintaining robust security is of utmost importance.
4. Proper key management is crucial for ensuring the secure operation of cryptographic protocols. This includes tasks such as generating, distributing, and revoking cryptographic keys. It is crucial to prioritize the maintenance of trust in certificate authorities (CAs) responsible for issuing digital certificates. This helps prevent certificate-related attacks and ensures the authenticity of cryptographic entities.
5. It is crucial for organizations that handle sensitive data to comply with regulatory requirements like GDPR, HIPAA, and PCI DSS. Communication protocols must comply with data privacy regulations and standards to ensure the confidentiality and integrity of personal and sensitive information.

Frequently Asked Questions

1. What do you understand by encryption?
2. How do you understand encryption algorithm?
3. What are the uses of encryption?
4. What are the types/methods of encryption?
5. What is the importance of secure communication protocols in cybersecurity?

CHAPTER SIX
INCIDENT RESPONSE BASICS

Overview

Chapter six talks about the incident response framework in cybersecurity. These responses help in mitigating the breaches posed by cyber criminals. Learn all about how to stop these security breaches in this chapter.

Introduction to Incident Response

In the ever-changing world of cybersecurity, where threats are constantly evolving and technology is advancing rapidly, having a strong incident response framework is crucial. The management and mitigation of security breaches, cyber-attacks, and other adverse events that compromise the confidentiality, integrity, or availability of information systems and data are encompassed by the incident response. It involves the implementation of processes and procedures to effectively handle these incidents. In today's interconnected world, where organizations heavily depend on digital infrastructure to carry out their operations, the significance of security incidents cannot be emphasized enough. When a cyber-attack occurs, it can result in significant financial losses, damage to reputation, penalties from regulators, and legal liabilities, among other serious consequences. In addition, the increasing prevalence of complex threats like ransomware, advanced persistent threats (APTs), and zero-day exploits highlights the importance of taking proactive steps to identify, control, and eliminate security incidents.

Incident Response Lifecycle

The incident response process usually adheres to a well-defined lifecycle, which includes multiple phases:

1. **Preparation**: The preparation phase focuses on establishing policies, procedures, and resources to ensure a smooth and efficient response to security incidents. Activities may involve the development of an incident response plan, the establishment of roles and responsibilities, the performance of risk assessments, and the implementation of preventive controls and safeguards.
2. **Detection and Analysis:** During the Detection and Analysis phase, security teams carefully monitor network traffic, system logs, and other sources of telemetry data to identify any potential security incidents. Further investigation is conducted into any suspicious activities or anomalies to ascertain their nature, scope, and impact on the organization's assets and operations.
3. **Containment**: After confirming a security incident, immediate action is taken to restrict its spread and mitigate any additional harm. It may be necessary to isolate affected

systems, disable compromised accounts, or block malicious network traffic. Preventing the incident from escalating and causing further harm to the organization is crucial.

4. **Resolution**: Once the incident is under control, security teams diligently work to address the root cause and restore affected systems to a secure state. Addressing these issues may involve fixing vulnerabilities, eliminating malware, or adjusting compromised devices. Thoroughly cleansing the environment is crucial to avoid any future incidents from happening again.

5. **Recovery**: During the recovery phase, the main objective is to bring back business operations to their normal state and retrieve any data that may have been lost or compromised. This could potentially require the restoration of backups, the rebuilding of infrastructure, and the implementation of extra security measures to avoid any future incidents. The objective is to reduce downtime and minimize the impact of the incident on the organization's operations and stakeholders.

6. **Lessons**: After resolving a security incident, it is essential to carry out a post-incident analysis to identify valuable insights and areas that can be enhanced. It may be necessary to review incident response procedures, update security controls, and implement training and awareness programs for staff. This process can provide valuable insights to improve the organization's security and better prepare for future threats.

Challenges and Considerations

Although incident response frameworks offer a systematic approach to handling security incidents, organizations frequently encounter a range of challenges during their implementation:

1. **Complexity of Attacks**: The complexity of cyber-attacks is on the rise, making it difficult to effectively detect and mitigate them. Attackers can utilize sophisticated methods, including polymorphic malware, encryption, and evasion tactics, to circumvent conventional security measures.

2. **Resource Constraints**: Numerous organizations face challenges when it comes to dealing with limited resources, such as budget, expertise, and technology, to efficiently detect and respond to security incidents. Their ability to deploy robust security controls, conduct proactive threat hunting, and retain skilled cybersecurity professionals may be hindered.

3. **Legal and Regulatory Compliance**: Ensuring legal and regulatory compliance can complicate incident response efforts due to the multitude of laws, regulations, and industry standards that must be considered. Organizations face the challenge of complying with legal and regulatory requirements when it comes to data breach notification, evidence preservation, and privacy protection while addressing security incidents.

4. **Collaboration**: Effective incident response often involves the coordination and collaboration of various teams and stakeholders, such as IT, security, legal, communications, and executive leadership. Effective communication and collaboration are crucial for promptly and efficiently addressing security incidents.

5. **Evolving Threat Landscape:** The cybersecurity threat landscape is always changing, as attackers constantly come up with new tactics, techniques, and procedures (TTPs) to exploit vulnerabilities and avoid detection. Organizations must remain alert and adjust their incident response strategies to effectively tackle new and evolving threats.

Effective Strategies for Incident Response

Organizations can greatly improve their incident response capabilities by implementing the following best practices:

1. **Create an Incident Response Plan**: Craft a thorough incident response plan that clearly defines roles, responsibilities, procedures, and communication protocols for effectively addressing security incidents. It is important to regularly review, update, and test the plan to keep up with changes in the threat landscape and the organization's evolving needs.
2. **Create a Rapid Response Team**: Gather a specialized incident response team consisting of highly skilled professionals from different fields, such as IT, security, legal, and communications. Ensure the team is equipped with the necessary authority, resources, and training to promptly and effectively address security incidents.
3. **Implement Security Controls**: Deploy a comprehensive defense strategy that includes a range of security controls to identify and address security incidents at different stages of an attack. These may include network firewalls, intrusion detection systems (IDS), endpoint protection, security information and event management (SIEM), and threat intelligence feeds.
4. **Ensure Regular Training and Drills:** Implement continuous training and awareness programs for employees to enhance their knowledge of common security threats, incident response best practices, and their roles and responsibilities during a security incident. Regularly conduct tabletop exercises and simulated cyber-attack drills to test the organization's incident response capabilities and identify areas for improvement.
5. **Establish Incident Reporting and Escalation Procedures:** Implementing clear procedures for reporting security incidents is crucial. It is important to establish channels for reporting, escalation paths, and criteria for severity classification. Promote a culture of openness and responsibility, fostering an environment where employees are confident in reporting any suspicious activities or security concerns, free from any potential consequences.
6. **Leverage Threat Intelligence**: Stay informed about the latest cyber threats, vulnerabilities, and attack trends by leveraging threat intelligence from reputable sources, such as industry information-sharing groups, government agencies, and commercial security vendors. Utilize threat intelligence to bolster threat detection, prioritize response efforts, and take proactive measures to safeguard against emerging threats.

Incident Handling Process

The incident handling process is a well-structured approach to detect, respond to, and recover from cybersecurity incidents. This process entails a well-coordinated set of actions that focus on identifying the incident's nature and extent, containing its spread, minimizing its impact, and restoring normal operations. Let's dive into the essential elements of the incident handling process and discuss the most effective ways to implement it.

1. **Preparation**

Proper preparation forms the bedrock of efficient incident handling. The process includes the establishment of policies, procedures, and resources required to promptly and efficiently address cybersecurity incidents.

Activities in this phase include:

- **Developing an incident response plan:** Organizations must establish a thorough incident response plan that clearly defines the roles and responsibilities of team members, outlines escalation procedures, establishes effective communication protocols, and identifies the technical resources that can be used to effectively respond to incidents. It is important to regularly review and update the plan to ensure it remains relevant to the evolving threat landscape and organizational structure.
- **Forming a response team**: It is crucial to gather a group of professionals who specialize in cybersecurity, IT operations, legal affairs, and communications to effectively handle incidents. Regular training for the team on incident handling procedures is essential, along with providing them with the necessary tools and resources to effectively investigate and mitigate incidents.
- **Conducting risk assessments**: Regularly assessing cybersecurity risks and vulnerabilities is crucial for organizations to identify potential threats and prioritize mitigation efforts. It involves assessing the security status of crucial systems, identifying possible attack routes, and evaluating the potential consequences of various incidents.
- **Implementing monitoring and detection mechanisms:** It is crucial to have strong monitoring and detection mechanisms in place. This includes using tools like intrusion detection systems (IDS), security information and event management (SIEM) systems, and endpoint detection and response (EDR) solutions. These tools help to identify and notify about any suspicious activities or potential security breaches.

2. **Detection and Analysis**

The detection and analysis phase commences once an incident is detected or suspected. The process includes identifying indicators of compromise (IOCs), analyzing the scope and impact of the incident, and determining the necessary response actions.

Activities in this phase include:

- **Incident triage:** Upon detecting an incident, it is essential to assess its severity, impact, and response priority. Gathering information about the incident is crucial, including details about the type of attack, the systems or data that were affected, and the potential risk to the organization.

- **Forensic analysis:** Using forensic analysis techniques allows for the collection and preservation of evidence about the incident, including log files, network traffic, and memory dumps. The evidence provided can greatly assist investigators in gaining a comprehensive understanding of the incident, as well as in effectively identifying the individuals responsible. Furthermore, it can serve as valuable support for any necessary legal or disciplinary measures that may need to be taken.
- **Analyzing the root cause:** After successfully containing and mitigating the incident, it is crucial to conduct a thorough analysis to understand how it occurred and uncover any vulnerabilities or weaknesses in the organization's defenses. This information can help guide future enhancements to security controls and procedures.

3. **Containment, Eradication, and Recovery**

After analyzing the incident, the main priority becomes containing its spread, eliminating the threat, and restoring affected systems and data to a secure state.

Activities in this phase include:
- **Containment**: Containment focuses on isolating affected systems and preventing the incident from spreading to other parts of the network. Procedures may include isolating compromised devices from the network, deactivating user accounts, or implementing temporary security measures to restrict the attacker's access.
- **Eradication**: The process of eradication entails identifying and eliminating the root cause of the incident, as well as removing any remaining malware or unauthorized access. It may be necessary to restore systems from backups, apply security patches or updates, and implement additional security controls to prevent similar incidents in the future.
- **Recovery**: Restoring affected systems and data to normal operations is a crucial part of the process. The process may include recovering data from backups, rebuilding compromised systems, and ensuring that all security controls are operating effectively. It is crucial to give priority to critical systems and data during the recovery process to minimize downtime and restore business continuity.

4. **Post-Incident Activities**

After the incident has been contained and normal operations are back on track, it is crucial to carry out a comprehensive review of the incident handling process. This will help us identify valuable lessons and areas that can be improved upon.

Activities in this phase include:
- **Incident debriefing:** A post-incident debriefing is essential to evaluate the organization's response to the incident, identify any areas for improvement in the incident handling process, and gather valuable insights for future incidents. It may be necessary to gather feedback from incident responders, carefully document key findings, and make appropriate updates to incident response procedures.
- **Documentation and reporting:** A thorough report should be created to document the incident, including its cause, impact, and the actions taken in response. This report can be shared with internal stakeholders, external partners, or regulatory authorities, depending on the incident's nature and applicable legal or compliance requirements.

- **Continuous improvement:** The incident handling process should be regularly reviewed and updated to incorporate lessons learned from past incidents, adapt to changes in the threat landscape, and leverage advancements in cybersecurity technologies and practices. Regular tabletop exercises, penetration testing, and security audits are essential to evaluate the organization's incident response capabilities and pinpoint areas for enhancement.

Roles within the Incident Response Team

In the ever-changing world of cybersecurity, where threats are constantly evolving, organizations must have the ability to quickly respond to incidents to minimize damage and safeguard their assets. IR teams are crucial in the incident response process, as they ensure that breaches are promptly identified, contained, and resolved.

The effectiveness of an IR team relies heavily on the clear definition of roles and responsibilities within the team.

1. **Incident Commander**: The Incident Commander is the person in charge of leading every incident response effort. This person is responsible for overseeing the response process, making important decisions, and coordinating the team's efforts. The IC should have excellent leadership qualities, the ability to make decisive decisions, and a thorough understanding of the organization's security posture. During an incident, the primary objectives of the Incident Commander (IC) are:
- Evaluating the seriousness and consequences of the incident.
- Organizing the required resources and personnel efficiently.
- Establishing effective communication channels with stakeholders.
- Regular updates are provided to executive management and relevant stakeholders.
- Ensuring adherence to regulatory requirements and internal policies.

The Incident Commander (IC) plays a crucial role in ensuring effective communication and coordination among all parties involved in the incident response process.

2. **Incident Responder:** Incident Responders play a crucial role in promptly investigating and effectively mitigating security incidents as they arise. The individuals have extensive technical knowledge in various areas including network security, forensics, malware analysis, and intrusion detection. Their duties consist of:
- Identifying and analyzing indicators of compromise (IOCs) to determine the nature and scope of the incident.
- Addressing and eliminating the threat to minimize any additional harm.
- Conducting forensic analysis to gather evidence for post-incident investigation and remediation.
- Taking steps to enhance security measures and safeguards to avoid any future occurrences.
- Working together with team members and external partners to exchange intelligence and best practices.

Incident Responders need to excel in high-pressure situations and quickly adjust to ever-changing circumstances. This is crucial because incidents can escalate rapidly, demanding immediate and decisive responses.

3. **Forensic Analyst:** The role of a Forensic Analyst is vital in the post-incident phase. Their main focus is to conduct thorough forensic analysis, reconstruct the timeline of events, determine the root cause of the incident, and collect evidence for potential legal proceedings. Forensic analysts are responsible for a variety of key tasks:

- Gathering and safeguarding volatile data from impacted systems.
- Performing disk and memory forensics to uncover evidence of malicious activity.
- Examining log files, network traffic, and other digital artifacts to track the actions of the attacker.
- Compiling findings and creating detailed reports for internal stakeholders and law enforcement agencies.
- Offering expert testimony in legal proceedings, if necessary.

Forensic Analysts need to have a deep understanding of digital forensic techniques, along with a comprehensive knowledge of the laws and regulations surrounding data privacy and chain of custody.

4. **Communications Coordinator**: It is crucial to prioritize clear and efficient communication during incident response efforts to keep stakeholders informed, coordinated, and reassured throughout the process. The Communications Coordinator oversees the management of both internal and external communications, which include:

- Establishing communication protocols and procedures for disseminating information to stakeholders.
- Handling media relations and overseeing public relations during high-profile incidents.
- Consistently keeping employees, customers, and regulatory authorities informed to uphold transparency and trust.
- Facilitating communication between the incident response team and executive management, ensuring that important information is conveyed and issues are addressed promptly.
- Keeping a close eye on social media channels and online forums to identify any potential misinformation or speculation regarding the incident.

The Communications Coordinator should have excellent interpersonal skills, expertise in crisis communication, and the ability to effectively communicate complex technical information.

5. **Legal Counsel**: It is crucial to address legal considerations when dealing with incident response, especially in situations involving data breaches or regulatory non-compliance. The role of the Legal Counsel is crucial in guiding the incident response team regarding legal obligations, liability risks, and compliance requirements. These are the responsibilities:

- Evaluating the legal consequences of the incident, such as possible regulatory fines, lawsuits, and harm to reputation.
- Guiding notification requirements following relevant data protection laws and regulations.

- Coordinating with external legal advisors and law enforcement agencies, as needed.
- Reviewing and drafting incident response documentation, including breach notification letters and settlement agreements.
- Offering advice on how to protect attorney-client privilege and keep sensitive information confidential.

Legal Counsel should possess a strong grasp of applicable laws and regulations, along with practical expertise in managing data privacy and cybersecurity issues.

Techniques for Detecting and Analyzing Incidents

Identifying unauthorized activities or security breaches within an organization's network or systems is a crucial aspect of incident detection. Effective proactive detection is essential in mitigating the consequences of cyber threats, as it allows for quick response and containment. The detection of incidents in the past heavily relied on signature-based detection methods, which were used to identify familiar patterns of malicious behavior. **Nevertheless, due to the ever-changing landscape of cyber threats, these methods have lost some of their effectiveness in identifying new types of attacks.**

- **Effective Advanced Threat Detection Techniques:** Organizations are increasingly adopting advanced threat detection techniques to effectively combat emerging cyber threats. These techniques utilize machine learning, artificial intelligence, and behavioral analytics to identify irregularities that may suggest malicious behavior. Machine learning algorithms can analyze large volumes of data to identify patterns and anomalies, which allows for the detection of threats that have not been encountered before. Behavioral analytics, in contrast, center around comprehending standard user behavior and identifying anomalies that could suggest a security breach.
- Both **Intrusion Detection Systems (IDS)** and **Intrusion Prevention Systems (IPS)** play a crucial role in an organization's cybersecurity infrastructure. The IDS system diligently monitors network traffic, keeping a watchful eye for any signs of suspicious activity. It promptly generates alerts whenever potential threats are detected, such as unauthorized access attempts or unusual data transfers. IPS takes proactive measures to block malicious traffic and prevent security breaches in real-time. Deploying IDS and IPS solutions can significantly enhance an organization's defense against various cyber threats, such as malware infections, phishing attacks, and denial-of-service (DoS) attacks.

Given the rise of remote work and the growing number of endpoints connected to corporate networks, organizations are increasingly concerned about endpoint security. Endpoint Detection and Response (EDR) solutions offer real-time monitoring and threat detection capabilities at the endpoint level, enabling organizations to swiftly identify and address security incidents. The solutions offered are designed to gather and analyze data from endpoints to identify any potentially concerning activity, such as unauthorized access attempts, file tampering, and unusual system changes. Through the integration of EDR and centralized threat intelligence and response capabilities, organizations can enhance their ability to protect endpoints from sophisticated threats. SIEM solutions are crucial for detecting and analyzing cybersecurity incidents, making them an essential component of any security strategy. The SIEM platforms gather and analyze data from different sources, including network logs, system logs, and security devices, to offer a comprehensive overview of an organization's security status. Through the analysis of events and the recognition of patterns that may indicate security incidents, SIEM solutions empower organizations to enhance their threat detection and response capabilities. In addition, SIEM platforms provide advanced features that can enhance cybersecurity operations, including threat intelligence integration, automated incident response, and forensic analysis capabilities.

Effective Threat Intelligence Integration: The integration of threat intelligence into incident detection and analysis processes is crucial to proactively address the ever-changing landscape of cyber threats. Threat intelligence offers valuable insights into emerging threats, malicious actors, and attack techniques, empowering organizations to proactively identify and address potential risks. By utilizing threat intelligence feeds from trusted sources like government agencies, cybersecurity vendors, and industry consortia, organizations can improve their capacity to detect and respond to cyber threats with greater effectiveness. Threat intelligence integration enables organizations to connect security events with established indicators of compromise (IOCs) and detect potential security incidents before they escalate. Effective incident detection is essential for a comprehensive incident response plan and the ability to conduct thorough forensic analysis. Effective incident response requires following predefined procedures and protocols to promptly contain and mitigate security incidents. Establishing clear roles and responsibilities within organizations can greatly streamline the incident response process and effectively minimize the impact of cyber threats. Forensic analysis is essential for investigating security incidents, determining the cause of breaches, and collecting evidence for legal and regulatory purposes. Through comprehensive forensic analysis, organizations can gain valuable insights from previous incidents and enhance their cybersecurity defenses to mitigate future threats.

Identifying Indicators of Compromise (IOCs)

IOCs are artifacts or observable patterns that indicate a security incident has taken place or is currently happening. The indicators can cover a wide range of suspicious network traffic and anomalous system behavior, indicating different types of cyber threats such as malware infections, unauthorized access, and data exfiltration. **There are various categories in which IOCs can be classified, such as:**

1. **File-based IOCs**: They encompass various indicators such as hashes of malicious files, filenames, file paths, and digital signatures linked to known malware or suspicious software.
2. **Network-based IOCs**: This category includes network traffic patterns, such as abnormal data flows, connections to suspicious IP addresses, or communication over non-standard ports.
3. **Host-based IOCs**: Signs of compromise can be detected on a specific host or endpoint, including unexpected system modifications, unauthorized processes running in memory, or unusual registry changes.

4. **Behavioral IOCs:** Indicators of compromise can be identified through behavioral anomalies, such as repeated login attempts, unauthorized privilege escalation, or abnormal data access patterns.
5. **Artifact-based IOCs**: These encompass various traces left by an attacker, like log entries, error messages, or remnants of tools utilized during an intrusion.

Through careful analysis of these indicators, cybersecurity professionals can gain valuable insights into potential security incidents and take the necessary steps to mitigate risks and safeguard their organization's assets.

Identifying Signs of Compromise

Appropriately identifying IOCs necessitates the utilization of cutting-edge technology, expert human knowledge, and a proactive approach to threat intelligence. The involvement of human analysts is crucial in complementing automated security tools and algorithms. They provide contextual analysis, anomaly detection, and the ability to identify emerging threats that may go undetected by automated systems.

1. **Integrating Threat Intelligence**

By incorporating threat intelligence feeds into security systems, organizations can ensure they are constantly informed about the most recent threat actors, tactics, and IOCs present in the cybersecurity landscape. Through the utilization of threat intelligence platforms and services, security teams can enhance their understanding of potential threats and improve their ability to proactively identify indicators of compromise (IOCs).

2. **Contextual Analysis**

It is crucial to grasp the context in which IOCs appear to differentiate between real threats and false positives. Security analysts need to thoroughly investigate the details surrounding each IOC, such as the systems that were impacted, user activities, and possible attack vectors. Through the correlation of various IOCs and contextual information, analysts can gain a more comprehensive understanding of the threat landscape. This enables them to identify complex attack campaigns that may involve multiple stages and vectors.

3. **Behavioral Analytics**

Machine learning algorithms are used by behavioral analytics platforms to analyze user and entity behavior across an organization's network. These platforms can detect deviations that may indicate potential compromise by establishing baseline behaviors for users, devices, and applications. Behavioral analytics not only improves IOC recognition but also empowers proactive threat hunting by identifying unusual activities that may not align with known IOCs.

4. **Endpoint Detection and Response (EDR)**

EDR solutions offer immediate insight into endpoint activities and facilitate swift response to security incidents. Through the monitoring of endpoint behavior, the collection of forensic data, and the application of behavioral analysis algorithms, EDR solutions can detect IOCs that suggest endpoint compromise. These indicators include fileless malware execution, lateral movement, and attempts to escalate privileges.

5. **Human Expertise**

Although automated threat detection technologies have made significant progress, human expertise is still crucial for identifying intricate IOCs and emerging threats. Security analysts have the expertise, analytical abilities, and intuition required to identify subtle signs of compromise that might go unnoticed by automated systems. By engaging in ongoing training, fostering collaboration, and actively sharing information, security teams can enhance their capacity to identify IOCs and swiftly address emerging cyber threats.

The Significance of Human Involvement

Automated tools and algorithms are highly effective at detecting known IOCs and patterns, but they are not without their limitations. Cyber adversaries are constantly adapting their tactics, techniques, and procedures (TTPs) to outsmart traditional security measures and avoid being detected. The role of human intervention is essential in this ongoing game of strategy, as it brings the adaptability, creativity, and critical thinking needed to outsmart highly skilled opponents.

1. **Flexibility**

Cyber adversaries utilize a range of tactics and techniques to bypass security controls and hide their actions. Keeping up with these ever-changing threats can be a challenge for automated detection mechanisms, as they depend on pre-established rules and signatures to detect familiar indicators of compromise. Human analysts, on the other hand, can adjust to different situations and use their cognitive skills to identify subtle anomalies and deviations that may indicate new attack methods or strategies.

2. **Innovation**

Cybersecurity demands a level of ingenuity and outside-the-box thinking to stay one step ahead of adversaries and effectively combat their tactics. The expertise of human analysts lies in their ability to approach threat detection and response with a creative mindset. They are skilled at exploring unconventional avenues and hypothetical scenarios to uncover hidden indicators of compromise (IOCs) and vulnerabilities. By adopting an offensive mindset, security professionals can proactively detect possible indicators of compromise (IOCs) and strengthen defenses against evolving threats.

3. **Critical Thinking**

In the field of cybersecurity, critical thinking plays a vital role. Analysts are faced with the challenge of evaluating intricate situations, carefully considering evidence, and making well-informed decisions even in high-pressure scenarios. The significance of IOCs can be critically assessed by human analysts, who take into account factors such as context, intent, and potential impact on the organization. By conducting thorough analysis and rigorous hypothesis testing, security teams can effectively differentiate between harmless anomalies and actual signs of compromise. This helps to reduce the occurrence of both false positives and false negatives.

4. **Collaboration and Knowledge Sharing**

Cybersecurity is a field that greatly benefits from the power of collaboration, as it relies on the sharing of information, collective intelligence, and community collaboration. Through promoting a collaborative environment, security teams can tap into the wealth of knowledge and insights from industry peers, researchers, and threat intelligence analysts. By participating in forums, conferences, and information-sharing platforms, cybersecurity professionals have the opportunity to share knowledge, engage in discussions about emerging threats, and collectively improve their ability to identify IOCs.

Frequently Asked Questions

1. What do you understand by incident response?
2. What are the effective strategies for incident response?
3. How do you detect and analyse incidents?
4. How do you handle incident response?
5. How do you identify indicators of compromise?

CHAPTER SEVEN
CYBERSECURITY CONSIDERATIONS WHEN WORKING FROM HOME

Overview

When working in the digital space right from the comfort of your home, it is important to be extremely careful about cyberspace and the Internet as a whole because there are preying cybercriminals who are waiting to exploit you. In this chapter, learn about the cybersecurity considerations when working from home.

Introduction to Cybersecurity Considerations

The global outbreak of COVID-19 in early 2020 prompted a significant shift in the way people work, as a new, highly contagious disease emerged. In an unprecedented turn of events, governments worldwide implemented strict lockdown measures to combat a global pandemic, effectively preventing people from collaborating in traditional office settings. During this lockdown, thanks to technological advancements made in recent decades, many individuals were able to work remotely, unlike in previous lockdowns throughout history. The abrupt shift from a large number of employees working in the office to working remotely, with little time to prepare, resulted in numerous cybersecurity challenges. Furthermore, despite the initial expectations of business leaders, the remote-working phase turned out to be more long-lasting than anticipated.

Concerns about Network Security

One of the main concerns with working remotely is the security of the networks that remote employees use to access sensitive data. **If those networks are not properly secured, two potentially disastrous outcomes can arise:**
- There is a possibility of sensitive information being stolen without the knowledge of both the employee and the employer.
- Some user's devices may be compromised by malware or hackers, allowing them to infiltrate corporate devices and networks. Once inside, they can cause significant damage in various ways.

What are the common security risks associated with remote-worker networks?

Businesses typically have more robust firewalls compared to those found in consumer products. However, it's worth noting that many remote workers rely on consumer-grade routers without any additional firewalls. Is it wise for your employer to rely on a router that was purchased for a mere $19.99 on Black Friday five years ago? Similarly, the majority of consumers lack the knowledge to properly configure their routers or firewalls, resulting in them only using the most basic options available. Although more sophisticated options are available, people often neglect to implement proper intrusion detection systems and other security technologies in their homes. These types of offerings are not typically found in affordable routers. Many businesses have a wide range of security technologies in place at their perimeters. Firewalls within an organization can restrict certain outbound requests, while data loss prevention systems can prevent emails with sensitive materials from being sent if they are mistakenly attached to the messages. It is uncommon for remote workers to have access to such security functionality from their routers. By the way, do employers have any knowledge about the routers their employees use while working remotely, let alone whether the firmware of those routers is regularly updated? Can managers accurately assess if employees working remotely have conducted vulnerability scans effectively? In addition to the concern about the router's patch level and firmware, it is worth considering how many employers have taken the necessary steps to ensure that their employees have adequately secured their personal home-based Wi-Fi access points. Do employers know other individuals utilizing the home network and the purposes for which they are using it? Downloading games can pose a risk to computer security, as malware can easily be transmitted through network connections.

Although there have been suggestions about employers using a full tunneling virtual private network (VPN) to mitigate these risks, this type of VPN would require all Internet traffic from the user to be directed through the employer's network. Additionally, it would route all Internet requests through the employer's security systems at the perimeter. It is important to note that there are risks involved when connecting an employee's home network to the employer's network. This is because any malware or cyber threats present on the home network can potentially spread to the employer's network. Additionally, in the event of any connectivity issues on the employer's end, the employee is unable to work, even from a remote location.

What steps can be taken to mitigate these risks?

This is an ideal scenario where your employer would supply you with a second router that connects to your home router. This second router would create a separate work environment, with a different network segment, effectively isolating it from all other devices on the network. Assuming the setup is done correctly, the work network will have the capability to make outbound requests to the Internet. However, your home network will not have the ability to initiate requests to the work network. This configuration is an improvement over using just one router, but it still has its limitations. For instance, there is still the possibility of communication between the work network and the home network. Although there are methods to maintain security in such a configuration, there is a greater chance of making configuration errors that could compromise security.

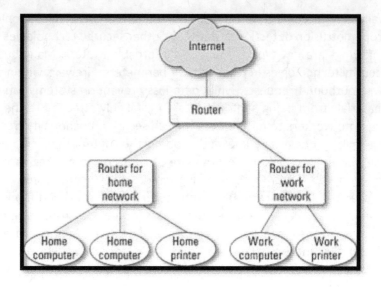

It is highly recommended that employees utilize computers provided by their employers. This practice not only ensures compliance with legal regulations regarding privacy but also minimizes the risk of data leaks and the exposure of corporate information on potentially insecure networks or devices. In an ideal scenario, only the employer's devices should be connected to the work network.

Concerns about Device Security

Devices that lack security measures can result in similar issues as vulnerable networks. This includes the risk of data theft and the potential for hackers to infiltrate the organization and cause various forms of damage. As previously stated, it is ideal for all work devices to be owned and managed by your employer.

There are numerous factors contributing to this:

- Employers should be aware of the contents of workers' devices to ensure optimal productivity and minimize distractions. This also helps to prevent any potential security breaches or malicious activities such as data theft.
- This scenario highlights the potential liability that employers may face when requesting employees to install apps on their devices. If these apps introduce vulnerabilities or cause conflicts with existing software, employers can be held accountable for the resulting problems.
- When an employee unexpectedly departs from the organization and still has work-related data on a personal device, there is a potential risk that this data could unintentionally or intentionally jeopardize the employer. If the device is stolen from the employee, the same principle applies. In a more extreme scenario, if an employee were to pass away, the

whereabouts of the employee's laptop, which contains sensitive work-related information, would be uncertain.

However, providing employees with employer devices to use from home may not always be a feasible option. Regardless of the type of computing device you use, be it a laptop, tablet, or smartphone, it is crucial to have the necessary security software installed, enabled, and regularly updated. Such devices need to have the capability of remote wiping in case of loss or theft. Additionally, all relevant data on these devices must be encrypted and properly backed up.

Cybersecurity Location

Although technology is commonly associated with data security, it is important to recognize that other factors also have a significant impact. The location where systems are used and data is accessed is another crucial factor to consider. The significance of this factor has greatly increased due to the shift from in-office working to remote working. It is now more crucial than ever to understand the dangers associated with location.

Shoulder surfing

An often overlooked threat to the security and privacy of employer data is posed by employees working remotely, despite its traditional nature. The exposure of sensitive information on an employee's device screen, visible to others or captured by cameras, can potentially compromise the confidentiality of the data. This issue is commonly referred to as shoulder surfing. Although not a novel idea, it continues to be a persistent issue. Particularly when a significant number of employees are anticipated to work outside of their regular professional environments. It is important to work from home if that is your designated work location, rather than choosing alternative places like coffee shops or public parks. In addition, it would be ideal to have a workspace that ensures your loved ones, including your children, cannot access any confidential information. If necessary, employers may also consider acquiring furniture or equipment to assist you in maintaining the desired level of privacy.

Eavesdropping

It is important to be cautious when it comes to voice communication. Avoid discussing sensitive information over the phone or any other voice communication system if there are other people around who can overhear you. The employees making these calls seemed completely unaware that they were unintentionally sharing private information that should have remained confidential. This sound machine that generates white background noise can be incredibly helpful when working from home. It's similar to the ones used by psychologists and psychiatrists to maintain privacy in their treatment rooms.

Theft

Home offices typically have lower security measures compared to professional office spaces, while public locations like parks, libraries, and coffee shops are even more vulnerable in terms of security. Remote workers, as a result, face a higher risk of laptop theft compared to their counterparts who work exclusively in traditional office settings.

Human error

It is crucial to recognize that when individuals experience frequent interruptions, their likelihood of making mistakes increases, which can ultimately result in data leaks. To ensure maximum productivity while working remotely, it is essential to establish a dedicated workspace that minimizes distractions. Undoubtedly, remote working locations pose more challenges compared to professional offices, especially during a pandemic when children are home all day and attending school virtually. It is important to establish a productive workspace that allows for efficient work, while also prioritizing focus and maintaining a reasonable level of data privacy.

Ensuring Cybersecurity in Video Conferencing

The shift from in-office work to remote work in 2020 due to the COVID-19 pandemic has led to a significant increase in the use of video call and conferencing technology. The number of individuals making work-related video calls from locations other than their official workplaces has grown exponentially in a short period. Given the swift and widespread adoption of this revolutionary and unfamiliar technology, it's important to acknowledge the potential risks that come with it. In the case of video conferencing, these risks specifically pertain to information security and privacy, which should not be taken lightly.

Ensure that personal items are not visible in the camera frame

During video conferences, it's important to be mindful of what's visible in your camera's frame and avoid displaying any sensitive or private information. It's important to note that mirrors and reflective surfaces in the frame can inadvertently reveal materials that are technically out of the camera's view during a video conference. If the preceding two points seem obvious, you can easily find numerous examples online of individuals who have failed to exercise caution. It would be beneficial to utilize a virtual background, especially if you have a physical green screen, as it helps to maintain the attention on you rather than any distractions in the background. Make sure to take advantage of the blur background features provided by your video conferencing tool. It is important to inform everyone in your home when you are participating in a video conference from home and your camera and/or microphone are on, even if it's only for a portion of the time. Please be aware that your camera feed and microphone are being shared, so others can hear or see you if you speak or walk near the device. Regrettably, numerous embarrassing incidents have occurred where individuals inadvertently entered the frame of someone else's video conference session while not fully clothed.

Ensure the security of your video conferences by preventing unauthorized access

Video conferencing cybersecurity encompasses a wide range of considerations beyond the mere exclusion of sensitive data from the frame. During the earlier months of the COVID-19 pandemic, numerous security violations occurred. Unauthorized parties would frequently join Zoom meetings and cause chaos, resulting in the creation and widespread use of a new term: Zoom bombing.

For a higher level of security in your video communications, take into account the following recommendations:

- Video conferencing should not be used for confidential discussions. Modern commercial video conferencing services are not suitable for highly confidential discussions. It's important to keep in mind that video conferencing software, just like any other software, can have vulnerabilities that can be exploited.
- Make sure to password-protect your sessions. Joining your video calls without authorization can be quite challenging for unauthorized users. Without the password, they won't have an easy time joining you.
- Make sure to create a new room name for each meeting. Certain video call services offer the convenience of reusing the same meeting room name repeatedly. Avoid doing this, as it increases the risk of someone with access to your call information joining another call.
- Consider using a waiting room. Several widely-used video-conferencing apps offer the convenient feature of automatically placing all participants in a virtual waiting room upon joining the call. As the host, you have the power to determine who enters the call meeting room from the waiting room. You can choose to admit everyone at once or selectively admit participants into the session. Participants who have pre-registered can be placed directly into the meeting room upon joining, while unknown parties seeking to join will have to wait for admission from the waiting room.
- Remember to always lock your sessions. After all the participants have joined a session, or if some haven't joined within a certain timeframe, the session will be locked to prevent any more parties from joining.
- Make sure to regularly check the list of participants in your meeting. If you come across anyone who doesn't belong, please remove them promptly! In addition, if there is an authorized participant who is causing disruptions during a video call session, it may be necessary to remove them. After locking the session, you should only need to review the list of participants once, immediately following the lock. It's important to keep an eye on the participant list if you have cohosts, as they may accidentally undo your locking.
- Turn off private chatting. If it's feasible, it would be great to have the option to prevent participants from sending private messages to each other through the video conferencing app. If they prefer to chat, they should utilize their usual chat applications.

- General participants should not be allowed to share their screens. If there is no specific requirement for a participant to share their screen in a virtual meeting, it is recommended to either disable screen sharing or limit it to only the host, yourself.

Concerns with Social Engineering

Individuals who work remotely, in isolated settings away from their coworkers, may be more susceptible to certain forms of social engineering attacks compared to those who work closely with their colleagues in a physical workspace. It can be challenging for individuals in different places to easily confirm the legitimacy of a request. When a homebound CFO receives a request from a CEO to issue a payment, they face the challenge of not being able to personally verify the legitimacy of the request by simply walking to the office next door. Furthermore, during the initial stages of the COVID-19 pandemic, numerous businesses had to swiftly transition to remote work without adequate preparation. Consequently, the technologies implemented in their physical offices to mitigate the risk of social engineering attacks were not effectively extended to remote locations before remote work began. It is crucial to emphasize to all remote workers that they are potential targets to effectively defend against social engineering attacks. Individuals who fully embrace this perspective tend to exhibit distinct behaviors in situations that may result in a data breach compared to those who do not share the same understanding. Training and assessments can also be beneficial in this regard.

Regulatory Concerns

Despite the need for remote work due to the rapid spread of a dangerous virus, it is important to remember that various laws and regulations related to information security and privacy still apply. It is important for businesses that fall under Europe's General Data Protection Regulation (GDPR) to prioritize the protection of personal information, even when implementing remote working practices. Similarly, it is important to note that even if a medical facility permits its clerical staff to work remotely on tasks like billing insurance companies for services, it is still obligated to comply with the data protection requirements outlined in the Health Insurance Portability and Accountability Act of 1996 (HIPAA). The United States. The rules set by the Securities and Exchange Commission (SEC) must still be followed. It is crucial to prevent the unauthorized disclosure of insider information, even to authorized parties at inappropriate times. Other regulations and industry guidelines follow the same principle. Ensure that your remote working program complies with all regulatory requirements to avoid any potential legal issues for yourself or others.

Frequently Asked Questions

1. What are the concerns about network security?
2. How do you ensure cybersecurity in video conferencing?
3. What are the concerns with social engineering?

CHAPTER EIGHT
SECURING YOUR ACCOUNTS

Overview

This chapter talks about how you can secure your accounts from cybercriminals and cyber-attacks.

Account Safety

People are often the weakest link in the cybersecurity chain, and it's important to recognize that the greatest threat to your cybersecurity is often yourself. Additionally, members of your family can also pose a significant risk. Although having extensive technology and technical knowledge is important, it is equally crucial to acknowledge and address the limitations of human nature. It is important to recognize that you are a potential target for cyber-attacks. Malicious individuals are determined to infiltrate your computer systems, electronically accessible accounts, and any other valuable information they can find. It is crucial to fully embrace the understanding that you are a target, even if you are already aware of it. Individuals who acknowledge the potential threat of criminals attempting to breach their computers and phones tend to exhibit different behaviors compared to those who are unaware of this reality. The latter group's lack of skepticism can sometimes result in unfortunate consequences. Understanding a concept intellectually is one thing, but fully embracing it is another. To ensure your security, it is crucial to truly believe that you are a potential target, rather than merely acknowledging the possibility in theory. It's important to make sure your family members are aware that they can also be targeted and have an impact on your digital security.

It's important to be aware of the potential risks your children may face online. Their actions can have unintended consequences, not just for themselves, but for you and the rest of the family too. There have been instances where attackers have successfully targeted individuals' employers through compromised remote connections. This occurred due to children misusing computers on the same networks as the employees who were working remotely. Consider the potential dangers and significant harm that can arise from such attacks, especially at a time when a significant portion of the population is working remotely. This type of attack typically does not result in immediate theft of money or data. Instead, the concern lies in the potential harm that the attacker may inflict on the target. This harm could manifest in various ways, such as financial, military, political, or other advantages for the attacker, while potentially causing damage to the victim. The extent of the damage caused is often much worse than if the perpetrator had only been motivated by financial gain.

Ensuring the Safety of Your External Accounts

Probably, computer systems owned by various businesses, organizations, and governmental agencies store data on every individual residing in the western world today. The systems can be found in various locations, such as within the organizations' facilities, shared data centers, or virtual machines rented from third-party providers. In addition, certain data may be stored in cloud-based systems provided by a third party. It is worth noting that the data (or every copy of the data) may not always be located within the same country as the individuals who are the subjects of the data. Regardless, the data can be categorized and segmented into various categories, based on the specific aspects that pique one's interest.

A useful approach to analyze the data to enhance its security is to categorize it based on the following scheme:

- User-established accounts and the data they contain
- Data associated with organizations that a user has willingly and knowingly engaged with, but the user lacks control over the data
- Data held by organizations that the user does not know has any connection with
- Each type of data necessitates a distinct strategy to mitigate potential risks.

Ensuring the Protection of User Account Data

When you engage in online banking, shopping, social media, or even basic web browsing, you inevitably share various types of data with the entities you interact with. Establishing and maintaining an account with a bank, store, social media provider, or other online party grants you control over substantial amounts of data that the party holds on your behalf. You have limited control over the security of that data since it is not in your possession. However, it is crucial to have a genuine concern for safeguarding your data and not compromising the security measures put in place by the party responsible for hosting your account. Although each situation and account may have its unique attributes, certain strategies can be employed to ensure the security of your data when it is held by third parties. It is important to note that not all the ideas in the following sections will be relevant to every situation. However, by selecting the appropriate items from the menu and implementing them in your various accounts and online behavior, you can greatly enhance your chances of maintaining a high level of cybersecurity.

Engage in transactions with trustworthy individuals

Supporting small businesses is a commendable choice that should be encouraged. It is indeed true that numerous large firms have experienced significant security breaches. However, if you come across a lesser-known store offering a significant discount on the latest electronic gizmo you're searching for, exercise caution. There could be a valid explanation for the discount, or it could potentially be a fraudulent scheme. It is important to always review the websites of stores you are dealing with to ensure everything appears legitimate. Be cautious if anything seems suspicious.

Use official apps and websites

There have been discoveries of unofficial replicas of official apps in multiple app stores. When installing a banking, credit card, or shopping app from a specific company, it's crucial to ensure that you download the official app to avoid any potential risks from malicious impersonators. It is important to only download apps from trusted app stores like Google Play, Amazon AppStore, and Apple App Store.

Avoid installing software from untrusted sources

The malware can capture sensitive information from various programs and web sessions on the infected computer. It's important to be cautious when coming across websites that claim to provide free copies of movies, software, or other items that usually come with a price tag. There is a possibility that these offerings are stolen copies, and it's worth considering how the website operator is generating revenue - it could potentially involve the distribution of malware.

Avoid rooting your phone

If you own an Android phone, you might find yourself considering the idea of rooting it. The process of rooting grants you more control over your device. However, it's important to note that rooting can compromise the security features of your device and potentially expose sensitive information to malware from other apps, which can lead to compromises in your accounts.

Avoid sharing unnecessary sensitive information

It is important to exercise caution when sharing personal information and only provide it to those who have a legitimate need for it. As an illustration, refrain from providing your Social Security number to any online stores or doctors. Although it is frequently requested, it is not necessary. Remember that limiting the amount of personal information you share with others can help minimize the risk of data breaches and the potential for your information to be linked together.

Use payment services that eliminate the need to share credit card numbers

Various services such as PayPal, Samsung Pay, Apple Pay, and others provide a convenient way to make online payments without disclosing your credit card details to vendors. When a vendor experiences a breach, the likelihood of your account information being stolen and used for fraudulent activities, including identity theft, is significantly lower compared to situations where the vendor stores actual credit card data. In addition, reputable payment sites have dedicated teams of highly skilled information security professionals who work tirelessly to ensure the safety of their platforms. This level of expertise is often unmatched by vendors who accept these payments. Furthermore, numerous stores have embraced the convenience of accepting payments through near-field communication (NFC). This technology allows for seamless contactless communication between devices, enabling you to effortlessly make wireless payments by simply holding your phone near a payment processing device. This payment scheme offers enhanced security from a cybersecurity perspective compared to the traditional method of handing credit cards to a clerk. Additionally, it minimizes the potential health risks associated with exchanging cash or payment cards between individuals who may be carrying germs.

Consider using one-time, virtual credit card numbers when it is suitable

This feature is offered by certain financial institutions, enabling users to generate temporary virtual credit card numbers through an app or website. These virtual numbers can be used to make purchases on a real credit card account, without the need to disclose the actual credit card number to the merchant.

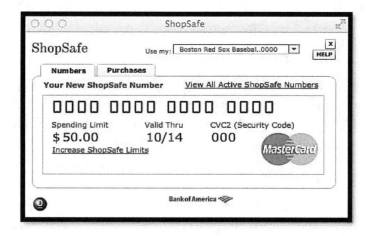

Although it may seem unnecessary to go through the process of generating one-time numbers, especially when you have a trusted vendor with reliable information-security measures, virtual credit card numbers can provide valuable protection against potential fraud. They can be particularly useful when dealing with unfamiliar parties. In addition to reducing the risk of dealing with corrupt vendors, virtual credit card numbers provide additional security advantages. This text is well articulated. If a vendor is hacked and your virtual credit card number, which was previously used, is stolen by criminals, they will be unable to make any charges with it. Their attempts to do so might assist law enforcement in locating them and aid forensic teams in identifying the origin of the credit card number data leak.

Keep a close eye on your accounts

Consistently monitor your payment, banking, shopping, and other financial accounts for any suspicious activities. It is important to thoroughly review your online transaction logs as well as your monthly statements, regardless of how they are delivered to you. Look for any unauthorized charges or unfamiliar transactions.

Report any suspicious activity as soon as possible

Reporting a case of fraud promptly to the relevant parties increases the likelihood of reversing it and stopping any further misuse of the materials involved. In addition, reporting the fraud as soon as possible increases the likelihood of apprehending the individuals responsible. Reporting potential cases of fraud and other forms of suspicious activity is crucial, so it's important to do so promptly.

Use a well-thought-out password strategy

Although it is commonly believed that complex passwords should be used for all systems, this approach proves to be ineffective in reality. Make sure to implement a strong password strategy.

Use multifactor authentication

Authentication methods for multi factor authentication include requiring a user to authenticate using two or more methods:

- Information that the user is familiar with, such as a password
- Something that the user possesses, such as a fingerprint
- A hardware token that the user possesses

It is advisable to employ authentication methods that offer greater security than relying solely on passwords, especially for highly sensitive systems.

Various forms of authentication serve different purposes:

- **Biometrics** refers to the utilization of measurements of different human characteristics to identify individuals. Various characteristics such as fingerprints, voiceprints, iris scans, facial structures, and typing speed can be used to differentiate individuals and determine their identity.
- **Digital certificates** are used to provide proof to a system that a specific public key belongs to the presenter of the certificate. The presenter's ability to decrypt messages encrypted with the public key in the certificate indicates that they possess the corresponding private key, which should only be held by the rightful owner.

- **One-time passwords**, or one-time tokens, can be generated by apps, read from a list of codes on a sheet of paper, or sent via SMS to your cell phone.
- **Hardware tokens** are usually compact electronic devices that offer various methods of generating or displaying unique numbers for authentication purposes. Today, smartphone apps can perform various functions, which mean that, in theory, a smartphone can act as hardware token. (It is important to note that smartphones can be susceptible to various security vulnerabilities that hardware tokens are immune to. Therefore, hardware tokens are generally more suitable for high-risk situations.)

- **Knowledge-based authentication** relies on genuine knowledge rather than easily guessable questions with limited answer options, such as "What color was your first car?"It's important to note that while knowledge-based authentication questions are often added to password authentication, this doesn't create multi factor authentication. This is because both the password and the knowledge-based answer are examples of things that a user knows. Nevertheless, implementing this approach can significantly enhance security if the questions are carefully selected.

It is highly recommended to utilize multi factor authentication, which is offered by many financial institutions, social media companies, and major online retailers. Consider that sending one-time passwords to users' smartphones via text messages may not always guarantee the security of the login process. Despite the initial assumption that this method verifies the possession of the smartphone, several vulnerabilities can compromise this assumption. There is a potential for sophisticated criminals to intercept text messages, even without having the necessary phone, or to hack into other chat applications used for transmitting such codes.

Remember to log out once you're done

It is not advisable to depend on automatic timeouts, closing the browser, or shutting down a computer to log out of accounts. Remember to log out manually each time you're done. It is important to ensure that you log out of your sessions when using a device that you are confident will remain secure.

Use your personal computer or phone

Consider the security of others' devices. For instance, a computer may have malware that can compromise your passwords and sensitive information, or even take control of your sessions and engage in malicious activities. In addition, it is worth noting that certain applications and websites continue to store data on endpoints that are used for accessing them, despite the significant issues this practice poses. It is important to ensure that your sensitive sessions do not leave behind any data for others to find.

Lock your PC

It is important to ensure the security of any computer used for accessing sensitive accounts. Make sure to lock the computer and keep it physically secure.

Using a separate, dedicated computer for sensitive tasks

It is advisable to invest in a dedicated computer solely for online banking and other sensitive tasks. While it may not be practical for everyone to have a second computer, there are certain security benefits to having a separate machine solely dedicated to tasks like reading email, accessing social media, and browsing the web.

Use a separate browser solely for tasks that require a higher level of security

Consider using a separate browser for sensitive tasks if you are unable to access a separate computer. Consider using a different browser for various activities such as reading the news, accessing social media, checking out blog posts, and more.

Ensure the security of your access devices

It is crucial to have security software installed on every device used to access secure systems. This software should be properly configured to conduct regular scans of newly added applications and perform periodic general scans. Additionally, it is crucial to regularly update the security software. Antivirus technology products are much more effective against newer strains of malware when they are kept up to date.

Ensure that your devices are always kept up to date

Regularly update your security software, as well as install operating system and program updates. This will help minimize your risk of being exposed to vulnerabilities. Using Windows AutoUpdate or a similar feature on other platforms can make this task much simpler for you.

Avoid conducting sensitive tasks while connected to public Wi-Fi networks

It is advisable to carry out any sensitive tasks in a location without access to a secure network over the cellular system, rather than relying on public Wi-Fi. There are numerous risks associated with using public Wi-Fi.

Avoid using public Wi-Fi in high-risk locations

Avoid connecting any device that you intend to use for sensitive tasks to a Wi-Fi network in areas that are known for cyber threats, such as hacking or malware distribution. Areas that are prone to digital poisoning include hacker conferences and countries with a reputation for cyberespionage, like China. It is advisable to keep your main computer and phone turned off and utilizes a separate set of devices when operating in these types of environments, according to numerous cybersecurity experts. This advice was frequently mentioned in the media leading up to the 2022 Winter Olympics in Beijing. Journalists covering the games and athletes participating in them openly discussed their strategies for addressing these concerns.

Make sure to access your accounts in secure locations

It is important to be cautious when using a private network and avoid typing passwords or performing sensitive tasks in public places where others can easily observe your actions.

Use suitable devices

Prioritize safety over cost when it comes to equipment. It is advisable to avoid buying electronics from sellers overseas and using unbranded networking devices that lack certification from U.S. authorities. There is a possibility that these devices may contain compromised hardware.

Establishing suitable boundaries

Several online platforms offer the option to set limits on certain transactions. These limits can include the maximum amount of money that can be transferred from a bank account, the largest charge that can be made on a credit card without physically using it (such as for online purchases), or the maximum quantity of goods that can be bought in a single day.

Use alerts

It is highly recommended that you take advantage of the text or email alert services offered by your bank, credit card provider, or favorite store. In an ideal scenario, receiving an alert from the issuer whenever there is activity on your account is highly desirable. From a practical standpoint, if this approach would be too much for you and lead to overlooking important messages (which is common for many individuals), you could alternatively request to receive notifications for transactions exceeding a specific dollar amount. This threshold can be customized for different stores or accounts, or any transactions that seem suspicious to the issuer.

Regularly monitor access device lists

Certain websites and apps, particularly those associated with financial institutions, provide the option to view the devices that have accessed your account. Regularly reviewing this list upon logging in can assist in promptly identifying any potential security issues.

Review the most recent login information

When you log in to certain websites and apps, particularly those related to financial institutions, you might come across details about your previous successful login sessions, including the time and location. Whenever any entity presents you with such information, give it a quick look. If there is any suspicious activity and someone has logged in pretending to be you, it will be easily noticeable.

Make sure to respond promptly to any fraud alerts

It is important to promptly respond if you receive a phone call regarding potential fraud on your account from a bank, credit card company, or store. However, refrain from engaging in conversation with the individual who contacted you. Instead, reach out to the outlet using a verified phone number that is prominently displayed on its official website.

Avoid sending sensitive information over an unencrypted connection

Make sure to check for the padlock icon when accessing websites, as it signifies the use of encrypted HTTPS. Today, HTTPS is widely used, with many websites implementing it, even if they don't require users to provide sensitive information. If the icon is not visible, it means that unencrypted HTTP is being used. If you find yourself in such a situation, it is best to refrain from sharing any sensitive information or logging in. It is concerning to see a site that requires a login and password or deals with financial transactions without a padlock, indicating a potential issue. On the other hand, it's important to note that the presence of the lock doesn't automatically guarantee the safety of the site, despite common misconceptions.

Be cautious of social engineering attacks

When it comes to cybersecurity, social engineering involves the manipulation of individuals by cyberattackers. These attackers use psychological tactics to trick their targets into taking actions or revealing confidential information that they wouldn't normally do. Many data breaches are initiated through social engineering attacks, which can be highly effective. It is important to be cautious when dealing with any form of communication, such as emails, text messages, phone calls, or social media interactions that claim to be from banks, credit card companies, healthcare providers, stores, and others. These could potentially be fraudulent and should be approached with skepticism. Avoid clicking on any links in such correspondence. It is important to always connect with such parties by entering the URL in the URL bar of the web browser.

Set up voice login passwords

There are other ways for criminals to gain unauthorized access to your accounts, not just through online means. Some criminals conduct online research and then manipulate their way into individuals' accounts by making phone calls to the customer service departments of the targeted organizations. For enhanced security, it is advisable to create voice login passwords for your accounts. These passwords need to be provided to customer service personnel for accessing your account information or making any modifications. Although many companies provide this capability, it is surprising that only a small number of people utilize it.

Ensure the security of your cell phone number

For optimal security, consider setting up a forwarding phone number to your cell phone and use that number when sharing your cell number. This will enhance the effectiveness of your strong authentication via text messages. By taking this precaution, the risk of criminals intercepting one-time passwords sent to your phone and the likelihood of other attacks are significantly reduced. For instance, Google Voice offers the option to set up a separate phone number that redirects calls to your cell phone. This allows you to provide a different number for general use while keeping your actual cell phone number reserved for authentication purposes.

Avoid clicking on links in emails or text messages

Links can often lead unsuspecting individuals to fraudulent websites, causing them to be diverted from their intended destination. Phishing emails and similar tactics are examples of social engineering attacks.

Ensuring the Security of Data Shared with Parties You've Interacted With

When you engage in online interactions, it's important to remember that not all of the data associated with your interaction is within your control. When you visit a website using standard web browser settings, that site can monitor your online activity. Due to the practice of content syndication, websites can monitor your activities on other websites, including those that are affiliated with advertising networks. To grasp the mechanics of this process, let's examine two distinct businesses with separate websites that use identical advertising networks. The businesses incorporate code into their websites, which enables the direct loading of advertisements from the ad network. When a user visits the first site, a cookie may be sent to the user's device by the ad network. This cookie can then be read by the same ad network when the user visits the second site, as both sites involve interaction with the ad network. When you log in to websites that track and syndicate content, they may have access to your true identity and a wealth of information about you, even if you haven't provided any personal details. Profiles of your behavior may be established and used for marketing purposes, even if you don't have an account or log in, without knowing your identity. (Naturally, if you ever log in to any site using the network in the future, all the sites with the profiles may link them to your true identity.)

Protecting data that is in the possession of third parties, but not under your control, can be quite challenging compared to safeguarding data in your accounts. However, it doesn't imply that you lack power. (Unfortunately, it is quite ironic and disheartening that the majority of data owners tend to prioritize the protection of personal information more effectively than the individuals themselves.) If Tor appears complex, you can also consider using a reliable VPN service for similar purposes. This technology enhances your browsing privacy by making it more difficult for websites to track your online activities. As a result, they are less likely to create detailed profiles about you, reducing the amount of personal data that can potentially be stolen. In addition, it may be undesirable for these parties to create profiles about you in the first place. The private mode offered by most web browsers, while not as effective as Tor or VPNs in preventing tracking, falls short of providing comprehensive protection. Regrettably, the private mode falls short of ensuring privacy and is plagued by several significant weaknesses.

Securing Data at Parties You Haven't Interacted With

It is quite surprising how various organizations possess substantial amounts of data about you, even though you have never intentionally engaged with them or permitted them to store such information. For instance, a prominent social media platform creates profiles for individuals who haven't signed up for an account yet. These profiles are based on mentions from others or interactions with websites that use social widgets or similar technologies. The service can utilize these profiles for marketing purposes, sometimes without knowing the person's true identity, and without the person being aware of the activities happening behind the scenes. In addition, various information services gather data from multiple public databases and create profiles using that information. These profiles may contain details that you may not be aware were publicly available. Genealogy sites often make use of various public records and provide the option for users to update information about individuals. There may be instances where subscribers to the site (or those with free trial subscriptions) can access various nonpublic information about you without your knowledge or consent, which can potentially create undesirable situations. These websites simplify the process of uncovering personal information like mothers' maiden names or birthdays, which can compromise the security measures implemented by various organizations.

In addition to family tree sites, several professional websites keep track of individuals' professional histories, publications, and more. Additionally, credit bureaus are responsible for storing a wide range of data regarding your credit activities. This information is provided to them by various financial institutions, collection agencies, and other entities. The Fair Credit Reporting Act provides some assistance in managing the information held by credit bureaus. However, it does not have the power to remove negative information from other sources, such as old newspaper articles that are available online. In addition to the privacy concerns involved, the presence of any information in those articles that can be used to answer authentication challenge questions can pose security risks. If you find yourself in such situations, it might be helpful to contact the data provider, explain the circumstances, and kindly request the removal of the data. There are instances where they will work together. Furthermore, certain businesses, like insurance companies and pharmacies, store and manage individuals' medical information. Usually, people have limited influence over such information. Undoubtedly, this kind of data, which is beyond your full control, can have an impact on you. It's important to note that numerous organizations may possess substantial amounts of information about you, even if you haven't had any direct contact with them.

Such organizations have a responsibility to safeguard their data stores, yet they often fail to do so adequately. The Federal Trade Commission highlights on its website that in 2017, a data breach at Equifax, a credit bureau, resulted in the exposure of sensitive personal information belonging to 143 million Americans. In situations where you are unable to manually update or request updates for records, there is limited action you can take to safeguard the data.

Ensuring Data Security by Avoiding Connection with Hardware of Uncertain Origins

Although technology has advanced significantly since the 1980s, the potential risks associated with connecting data storage media of uncertain origin to a computer remain unchanged. Connecting a USB drive with malware-infected files to your laptop can result in infecting your laptop. Infected contents on memory cards can cause significant cybersecurity issues for any device they are inserted into. Furthermore, whenever a hardware device is connected to a computer using a USB connection, it opens up the possibility for communication between the two devices. The way Plug and Play functions allows for the execution of specific code on a computer when a USB device is initially connected. However, if this code is compromised, there is a risk of being hacked. Other USB devices follow the same principle. This text highlights the potential dangers that can arise when connecting a device with compromised hardware or flash memory to a computer or a network. It emphasizes the serious risks that can be posed to both the connected computer and other devices on the same network. In addition, there are USB devices that can pose a risk to computers by causing damage. This type of device is designed to self-charge through the USB port and store the electricity in a capacitor. However, when it releases all the stored energy in one powerful burst, it can cause permanent damage to the connected electronics in less than a second. Phone chargers and similar devices can also present challenges. Any device that can be connected to a USB port can communicate with the USB-enabled device and potentially cause damage by overloading it with electricity. Remember to pack your chargers, USB drives, and memory cards when you're traveling.

Frequently Asked Questions

1. How do you ensure the safety of your external accounts?
2. How do you ensure the protection of use account data?
3. How do you secure your accounts generally?

CHAPTER NINE
COMPUTER SECURITY TECHNOLOGY

Overview

In chapter nine, the various computer security technology types will be discussed.

Computer Security Technology Overview

Hackers frequently use these tools to execute a range of hacks on networks or systems. These tools can assist you in evaluating the system and network, as well as detecting any vulnerability. These tools are used for analyzing system capabilities and identifying bugs during the testing phase of development. Hackers are often regarded as highly skilled individuals within the IT field. Exploiting a private computer and network system is more challenging than developing it. The term "**Hacking**" involves gaining unauthorized access to someone's system to steal sensitive information and cause harm to computer systems or networks. Hackers are well-versed in the workings, development, and architecture designs of the systems. This information will assist them in bypassing system security effortlessly to obtain the necessary information. Hacking also encompasses activities such as privacy invasion, unauthorized access to company data, online scams, and fraud. This provides insights into various tools that can assist you in gaining a deeper understanding of network and system vulnerabilities.

EtherPeek

This software is highly effective and compact, designed specifically for analyzing an MHNE (Multiprotocol Heterogeneous Network Environment). The functionality involves analyzing data packets on the specific network. The supported network protocols include IP, IP ARP, AppleTalk, TCP, NetWare, UDP, NBT Packets, and NetBEUI.

QualysGuard

This software suite consists of integrated tools that can effectively modify network security processes and reduce consent costs. The system is composed of various modules that collaborate to carry out the entire testing process, starting from the initial phase of mapping and analyzing attack surfaces to identify any security vulnerabilities. This tool effectively manages, identifies, and isolates global networks for enhanced network security. The text also offers valuable security intelligence and streamlines the auditing, monitoring, and protection of network systems and web applications.

SuperScan

An effective tool utilized by network administrators for scanning and analyzing TCP ports and projecting hostnames. SuperScan is highly intuitive thanks to its user-friendly interface. SuperScan performs the following operations: Scanning the port range can be done from the provided built-in list or any range defined by the user. Examine and evaluate the replies from connected hosts to the network. Performing scans to ping and check network ports across various IP ranges. Combine the list of ports to create a fresh one. Connect to any port that is currently available or open.

WebInspect

This is a web-based security assessment application that enables developers to identify both known and unknown vulnerabilities in the web application layer. The system is composed of various modules that collaborate to carry out the entire testing process, starting from the initial phase of mapping and analyzing attack surfaces to identify security vulnerabilities. The analysis involves checking the configuration of the webserver by attempting parameters injection, directory traversal, and cross-site scripting.

LC4

This application is commonly used in computer networks for password recovery. This software, commonly referred to as "L0phtCrack," is primarily utilized to assess password strength and retrieve Microsoft Windows passwords. It employs various techniques such as directory searches, hybrid attacks, and brute-force methods. The system is composed of various modules that collaborate to carry out the entire testing process, starting from the initial phase of mapping and analyzing attack surfaces to identify security vulnerabilities.

NMAP

This tool, known as "**Network Mapper**," is a powerful open-source tool used for network discovery and auditing. The main purpose of its development was to scan enterprise networks, keep track of network inventory, monitor network hosts, and manage network service schedules. It is used to induce: What types of hosts are available? What services do they offer? Could you please provide information about the operating system running on those hosts?

Metasploit

Metasploit is widely recognized for its exceptional capabilities in the field of exploitation. There are various versions available, each with its own set of features. This tool is versatile and can be used through both the command prompt and a user-friendly web interface to carry out a wide range of tasks. Penetration testing for small businesses. Explore, analyze, and incorporate network data. Take a look at the exploit modules and thoroughly test all exploits on network hosts.

Burp Suite

Burp Suite is widely recognized as the go-to tool for conducting security tests on web-based applications. The system is composed of various modules that collaborate to carry out the entire testing process, starting from the initial phase of mapping and analyzing attack surfaces to identify potential security vulnerabilities. The interface is designed to be easy to use, and administrators have the option to manually conduct system tests using various techniques.

Angry IP Scanner

This tool is capable of detecting IP addresses and scanning a wide range of ports across different platforms. You can easily find it on the internet. The multithreaded technique is utilized by administrators to efficiently scan a vast range of IP addresses by combining multiple scanners. It checks individual IP addresses.

Frequently Asked Questions

1. What do you understand by computer security technology?
2. What are the different computer security technologies?

CHAPTER TEN
CYBERSECURITY FOR BUSINESSES AND ORGANIZATIONS

Overview

In this chapter, you will learn how employing cybersecurity can benefit both businesses and organizations now and soon.

Ensuring Effective Leadership

When you have a network and multiple users, the responsibility for computer security becomes more complex. Someone within the business must take full responsibility for information security. That individual could be you, the business owner, or another person. However, it is crucial for the person in charge to fully comprehend their level of responsibility. Many small businesses choose to outsource certain day-to-day activities related to information security, allowing the person in charge to focus on other aspects of the cybersecurity function. Regardless, it is ultimately the responsibility of that individual to ensure that essential tasks, like timely installation of security patches, are carried out. It is not a valid excuse to say "I thought so-and-so was taking care of that security function" if a breach occurs. Unfortunately, we often hear people attempting to use this excuse, but it does not hold much weight.

Keeping an Eye on Employees

Small businesses often face significant challenges when it comes to managing their employees and the potential cybersecurity risks they pose. Data breaches are often caused by human errors. **Small business owners must prioritize employee education. Education is comprised of three essential components:**

- **Recognizing potential risks**: It is crucial to ensure that all employees are aware of the fact that they, along with the entire business, can be targeted. Individuals who hold the belief that criminals have intentions to infiltrate their computers, phones, and databases, or to unlawfully obtain their data, tend to exhibit distinct behaviors compared to those who have not embraced such realities. Although formal, regular training is preferred, even a brief conversation held when workers begin and reinforced with occasional reminders can provide significant value in this area.
- **Foundational information-security training**: All employees need to have a solid understanding of the basics of information security. The users should be aware of certain cyber-risky behaviors to avoid. These include refraining from opening attachments or clicking on links in unexpected email messages, downloading content from questionable

sources, using public Wi-Fi inappropriately, and purchasing products from unknown stores with suspiciously low prices and no publicly known physical address.

There are plenty of training materials available online that are related to the topic. However, it is important to remember that training alone cannot be relied upon as the only means of protecting against significant human risks. It's important to keep in mind that despite receiving clear training, many individuals continue to make unwise decisions. In addition, training fails to address the issue of employees who deliberately sabotage information security.

- **Practice**: Information security training should be practical and hands-on. It is important to provide employees with the chance to apply their knowledge, such as recognizing and taking action against potential phishing emails.

Motivate your staff

It is important to not only address employees' mistakes but also acknowledge and incentivize their efforts in maintaining a secure cyber environment and practicing good cyber hygiene. It is widely acknowledged that using positive reinforcement is highly effective and generally well-received than resorting to negative reinforcement. In addition, numerous organizations have effectively implemented reporting systems that enable employees to confidentially inform the appropriate authorities within the company about suspicious insider activities that may indicate a threat, as well as potential system bugs that could result in vulnerabilities. These programs are widely used by larger businesses, but they can also be advantageous for small companies and other organizations.

Be cautious about sharing sensitive information

Numerous instances exist where employees' errors inadvertently provide hackers with access to the organization's systems. Similarly, there have been numerous instances of dissatisfied employees engaging in data theft and/or system sabotage. The impact of such incidents can be devastating for a small business. Ensure the safety of yourself and your business by establishing a robust information infrastructure that can effectively mitigate any potential risks or damages. How is it possible to accomplish this? Ensure that workers have the necessary access to computer systems and data required for optimal job performance, while also implementing strict measures to prevent unauthorized access to sensitive information. It is important to restrict access to certain systems based on job roles. For instance, programmers should not have access to a business's payroll system, and comptrollers do not require access to the version control system that stores the source code of a company's proprietary software. Controlling access can have a significant impact on the extent of a data breach in case an employee becomes untrustworthy. Numerous businesses have experienced the consequences of this lesson through difficult experiences. Avoid becoming like them.

Provide each individual with their own set of login credentials

Every employee needs to have their login credentials for each system used by the organization. It is important to refrain from sharing your credentials. This scheme enhances the ability to audit individuals' activities in the event of a data breach or cybersecurity incident. It also motivates individuals to take better care of their passwords, as they are aware that any misuse of their accounts will be addressed directly with them by management. When employees know they will be held accountable for their actions regarding security, it can have a positive impact on their proactive behavior. In addition, each individual needs to have multi factor authentication capabilities, such as a physical token or a code generated on their smartphone.

Limit the access of administrators

System administrators usually have superuser privileges, which allow them to access, read, delete, and modify other people's data. It is crucial, therefore, for business owners to implement controls to monitor the actions of administrators, especially if there are multiple superusers. As an illustration, it is possible to record administrator actions on a separate machine that is inaccessible to the administrator. Limiting access to a particular machine in a specific location can be an alternative approach, although it may not always be feasible due to business requirements. This method involves positioning a camera to capture the actions of the administrator on that machine.

Restrict access to corporate accounts

Your business may have multiple accounts of its own. For instance, it could include social media accounts like a Facebook page, Instagram account, and Twitter account, as well as customer support, email accounts, phone accounts, and other utility accounts. Only provide access to individuals who have a genuine need for it (refer to the previous section). Each person you grant access to must-have easily traceable access, allowing you to easily identify who made changes to the account. Achieving basic control and audibility on Facebook Pages is straightforward. For instance, you can take ownership of the Facebook Page for your business and permit others to contribute to the page. In certain situations, granular controls may not be accessible, leaving you with the choice of either granting multiple individuals access to a social media account or having them submit content to a single person (possibly yourself) who will then make the necessary posts. Ensuring that every authorized user of corporate social media accounts has their account for control and audibility becomes more challenging when considering the need for multi factor authentication to protect sensitive accounts. Certain systems provide multifactor authentication capabilities to accommodate the need for multiple independent users to have auditable access to a single account. In certain situations, systems that provide multifactor authentication capabilities may not seamlessly integrate into multi-person environments. For instance, they might enable the use of a single cell phone number to receive one-time passwords through SMS. When faced with such situations, you'll have to decide on whether to

- Use multifactor authentication but with a workaround. For instance, one way to handle this is by utilizing a VOIP number to receive the texts and setting up the number to forward the messages to multiple parties through email. This service, like the one provided by Google Voice, is free of charge.

- Make sure to use the multifactor authentication without any exceptions or bypasses. Adjust the settings on the authorized users' devices so that they are not required to use multifactor authentication for their activities.
- Use a form of multifactor authentication that does not require a workaround. For instance, a system that enables multiple users to authenticate separately using various credentials and multifactor logins, and then permits them to perform actions on the same account.
- Use a form of multifactor authentication that does not require a workaround, while still maintaining a consistent approach for all users. For instance, users can utilize distinct initial authentication credentials while still being able to use shared multifactor credentials. This can be achieved by providing them with a one-time code generator that is configured with the same seed, ensuring that it generates identical one-time codes at the same time.
- Choose not to use multifactor authentication and instead rely solely on strong passwords. This solution is not advisable.
- Consider exploring alternative solutions by making adjustments to your processes, procedures, or technologies used for accessing these systems.
- Incorporate third-party products that overlay systems. This is frequently the optimal choice when it is accessible.

Typically, the final choice is the most favorable one. The content management systems can be configured to accommodate multiple users, each with strong authentication capabilities. These users are granted auditable access to a single social media account. Although larger enterprises typically opt for this approach due to management and security considerations, it is common for small businesses to choose the simpler route and forego the use of strong, multifactor authentication in these situations. Considering the relatively low cost in terms of both money and time, it is highly recommended to explore third-party products before considering alternative approaches when it comes to implementing proper security. If you ever find yourself dealing with a disgruntled employee who had access to the company's social media accounts, or if a happy employee with such access gets hacked, the importance of having proper security with audibility will become evident.

Implementing employee policies

Every business, regardless of its size, must have an employee handbook that outlines the rules and regulations concerning the use of company technology systems and data.

- Employees are required to use technology in a responsible, appropriate, and productive manner to fulfill their professional duties.
- Company devices, company Internet access, and email provided to employees are intended for job-related activities. Employees may use the system for personal purposes as long as it does not violate any other rules outlined in this document and does not disrupt their work.

- Employees are expected to take full responsibility for any computer hardware and software provided by the company, ensuring that these items are protected against theft, loss, or damage.
- Employees are expected to take responsibility for the accounts provided by the company, ensuring that access to these accounts is properly safeguarded.
- Employees must not share any company-provided items used for authentication, such as passwords, hardware authentication devices, PINs, etc. It is their responsibility to ensure the security of these items.
- Connecting any networking devices, such as routers, access points, range extenders, and so on, to company networks is strictly prohibited for employees unless explicitly authorized by the company's CEO. In addition, it is important to note that employees are not allowed to connect personal computers or electronic devices, including Internet of Things (IoT) devices, to any company networks except for the Guest network. This policy is clearly outlined in the Bring Your Device (BYOD) policy.
- It is the employees' responsibility to ensure that security software is running on all company-provided devices. The company will provide the software, but it cannot guarantee that these systems will always function as expected. The deactivation or impairment of security systems by employees is strictly prohibited. If employees suspect any issues with the security systems, they should immediately inform the company's IT department.
- It is the employees' responsibility to ensure that security software is regularly updated. It is important to note that all company-issued devices are equipped with Auto-Update enabled, and employees must refrain from disabling this feature.
- Employees are expected to ensure that their devices are always updated with the latest operating system, driver, and application patches whenever vendors release them. All employees must keep the Auto-Update feature enabled on their company-issued devices.
- Engaging in any unlawful activity, regardless of its severity, is strictly forbidden. This rule applies to federal, state, and local laws, regardless of the location or time when the employee is bound by these laws.
- The employee is not allowed to store or transmit copyrighted materials belonging to any party other than the company or employee on company equipment without explicit written permission from the copyright holder. The company may transmit licensed material following the applicable licenses.
- The act of sending mass unsolicited emails (spamming) is strictly prohibited.
- Using company resources for tasks that do not align with the company's mission, even if they are not technically illegal, is not allowed. The content that is prohibited includes accessing or transmitting sexually explicit material, vulgarities, hate speech, defamatory materials, discriminatory materials, images or descriptions of violence, threats, cyberbullying, hacking-related material, stolen material, and more.
- Employees whose job involves working with such material are exempt from the previous rule, as long as they must carry out their duties. As an illustration, individuals in charge of setting up the company's email filter can communicate with each other about

119

incorporating different terms related to hate speech and vulgarities into the filter configuration, without breaking any rules.

- Devices with Wi-Fi or cellular communication capabilities must not be turned on in China or Russia without explicit written permission from the company's CEO. Loaner devices will be provided to employees who are traveling to those regions. Personal devices used in those regions cannot be connected to the Guest network or any other company network.
- Compliance with the company's Public Wi-Fi policies is required when using public Wi-Fi with corporate devices. In an ideal scenario, companies should prohibit such usage, except in exceptional and specific circumstances.
- Employees are required to back up their computers using the company's backup system, as outlined in the company's backup policy.
- Copying or backing up data from company devices to personal computers, storage devices, or cloud-based repositories is strictly prohibited for employees.

All passwords for systems used as part of an employee's job must be unique and not reused on any other systems. For enhanced security, it is recommended that passwords include a combination of three or more words, with at least one word not commonly found in the English dictionary. These words can be joined together with numbers or special characters.

Alternatively, passwords can also meet the following conditions:

- Make sure your password has at least eight characters, including at least one uppercase letter.
- Make sure to include at least one lowercase character.
- Include a numerical value
- Lack any words that can be found in an English dictionary
- Using the names of relatives, friends, or colleagues as part of a password is not allowed.

Ensure that data is encrypted before it is taken out of the office for business purposes. This applies to data stored on various types of media, such as hard drives, SSDs, CDs/DVDs, USB drives, or when transmitted over the Internet. Copying the document to employee cloud-storage accounts (such as Google Drive or Dropbox) is not permitted outside of the office. The business requires that all data taken from its infrastructure or contracted infrastructure be promptly returned or destroyed after remote use or upon termination of employment.

- During a breach, cybersecurity event, or any natural or man-made disaster, only the company's officially designated spokesperson is authorized to communicate with the media on behalf of the company.
- Devices that have been flagged by the FBI, the FCC, or other United States federal agencies as potentially unsafe or used for spying on Americans are strictly prohibited from being connected to any company network or brought into the physical offices of the company. It is crucial to avoid storing or processing company data on such devices.

Implement and uphold social media policies

It is crucial to have well-crafted, effectively implemented, and strictly enforced social media policies. This is because any inappropriate posts on social media platforms, whether by your employees or yourself, can cause significant harm and consequences. The potential consequences of their actions are significant, including the risk of sensitive information being leaked, compliance rules being violated, and criminals using their tactics to social engineer and attack your organization. This could expose your business to boycotts, lawsuits, and other negative outcomes. It is important to ensure that all employees have a clear understanding of the acceptable and unacceptable use of social media. It is advisable to seek legal counsel when formulating policies to ensure compliance with freedom of speech regulations. Consider incorporating technology to prevent social media from turning into a marketing nightmare.

Keep track of employees

Companies should inform users of their right to monitor employees' technology usage, regardless of whether they plan to do so. It is crucial to ensure that the admissibility of evidence is not challenged due to a lack of monitoring rights, especially in cases where an employee may engage in unauthorized data theft. In addition, informing employees about potential monitoring can help deter them from engaging in unauthorized activities, as they are aware of the possibility of being monitored during such actions. Monitoring should be limited to employer-issued devices and networks. The company has the authority to monitor and control all electronic communications, files, and network activity transmitted through its technology systems, whether onsite or offsite. The systems encompass both those that are owned and operated, as well as those that are leased, licensed, or have any other usage rights. In addition, it is important to note that all forms of electronic communication, including email, text messages, and voicemail, are considered to be official records of the company. These records may be subject to legal discovery or disclosure requests from regulators and other parties.

Managing a Remote Workforce

Although the idea of remote work is not a recent development, the global outbreak of the novel coronavirus in early 2020 has led to a significant increase in the number of individuals working from home. The COVID-19 pandemic has emerged as the primary driver for the shift towards remote working. The world underwent a rapid transformation, shifting from a time when people were mostly confined to working at their employers' chosen locations, to a time when a considerable portion of the population exclusively worked from home. Despite the gradual return to workplaces post-pandemic, a significant number of individuals continue to work remotely from home on certain occasions. Although working remotely during a global pandemic can provide safety from unseen microscopic threats and offer employers productivity and financial advantages, the need for remote workers to access crucial data and systems from uncontrolled environments raises significant cybersecurity issues.

Use work devices and separate work networks

When employees use their devices to connect to employer networks, access employer systems, or work with employer data, it exposes employers to significant risks. These risks include malware infections, insecure storage of data, unauthorized access by malicious individuals, and various other cybersecurity concerns. Employees should conduct remote work using computers and other computing devices provided by the employer. It would be ideal if access to employer systems could be conducted through Internet connections and networking equipment provided and managed by the employer. Furthermore, it is important to note that personal devices should not be connected. It would be beneficial for employers to have the capability to remotely access and monitor or wipe such devices if they are lost or stolen. In many cases, though, such arrangements are either impractical or impossible, and as a result, it is important to consider alternative precautions.

It would be beneficial for employers to provide employees with a network router if they plan on using their Internet connections. This way, employees can connect the router to their home network routers, effectively separating the employer's equipment and data from the main network segment at home and its traffic. It is strongly advised that employees refrain from connecting personal devices to employer networks. However, if for any reason you or your employer decide to disregard this advice, it is crucial to ensure that all devices connecting to the employer network have the latest security software installed. Employers need to take charge of software installations and be aware that if any software they ask employees to install causes technical problems on their devices, the employer may have to address the issue. It is important to never attempt to monitor an employee's actions on their devices.

Establish virtual private networks

Remote workers can enjoy several significant benefits with a virtual private network (VPN). This feature ensures that unauthorized parties cannot share the employer's Internet connection or access the contents of the VPN user's transmissions. It also protects against other parties on the local network and the Internet service provider from viewing the user's data. The use of a VPN to connect a separate network router to a corporate remote-worker network can be beneficial. This type of network, often referred to as a demilitarized zone (DMZ), is not fully trusted by the company but is not open to the public. It is particularly useful when users need to access multiple corporate devices from a remote location or when multiple employees are working at that location. If network-to-network VPNs are not feasible or if a single user is using a single device, it may be suitable to establish a direct connection from the user's remote corporate device. In certain situations, both types of VPN connections can pose cybersecurity risks, particularly if an employer lacks the necessary expertise or resources to effectively implement and monitor the VPN. It is highly recommended to keep work devices separate from personal devices by using a separate network at a remote location, even if a VPN is not being used.

While consumer-type VPN services are an option, they may not be the most ideal choice. Unlike a secure tunnel that connects the remote worker directly to the employer's infrastructure, these services connect the employee to the VPN provider's systems first and then communicate with others on the Internet. This introduces the possibility of potentially insecure transmissions. Employees shouldn't connect their devices to an employer's VPN. Enabling individuals to connect in this manner has the potential to result in a cybersecurity catastrophe.

Develop standardized communication protocols

Prioritize security when making decisions in this regard. The policies should include configuration requirements, such as the use of passwords for video calls, the implementation of virtual "waiting rooms" to control meeting attendance, and the restriction of non-public meetings to authenticated and signed-in users only.

Use a familiar network

It is important to ensure that any wireless network you connect to while working from home is encrypted and secured with a strong Wi-Fi key (WPA2 or better). It is important to follow this advice to protect your communications and ensure that you are connecting to the correct access point or router. It is important to be aware of the potential risks associated with hackers setting up "evil twin networks" that mimic your network. In some cases, your device may mistakenly connect to the malicious access point instead of the legitimate one, especially if the signal strength is stronger. By using Wi-Fi security, the chances of encountering a troublesome connection are greatly reduced. This is because it is highly unlikely that a hacker would have access to the same encryption key. (If an attacker somehow obtains your key, you will be facing more significant issues than just this connection.)

Find out how backups are managed

You need to have a well-executed plan for backing up the systems and data of remote workers. It is the responsibility of the employer to perform, manage, and administer backups. It is not advisable to depend on employees to back up employer data. It's important to exercise caution when choosing your remote work environment. Consider that working from home may have less security compared to a traditional professional work environment. This is not only due to technical reasons but also because of the individuals who are frequently present in these different settings. It is important to note that working remotely can present certain challenges, including the issue of "shoulder surfing." To mitigate this risk, it is recommended that remote employees primarily work from secure locations such as their homes, where access can be tightly controlled. It is advisable to avoid working from public places like coffee shops, airports, libraries, parks, sidewalks, or restaurants. Furthermore, despite the advantages of having employees work from home, there are still concerns about unauthorized individuals gaining access to sensitive information displayed on computer screens or overheard during phone calls. Many organizations understandably feel uneasy about the possibility of remote workers' family members or partners being privy to the confidential information handled and exposed during work-at-home sessions. Noise machines have been widely used by professionals like psychologists, psychiatrists, and social workers to create a barrier between treatment rooms and waiting areas, ensuring confidentiality. Similarly, these machines are also popular among individuals who use them to generate soothing background noise that aids in falling asleep. Furthermore, privacy screens for laptops can significantly decrease the chances of unauthorized individuals being able to view the contents displayed on the screen. This type of screen ensures that the displayed contents are easily visible when viewed head-on, but become less visible when viewed from an angle.

Remain highly cautious when it comes to social engineering tactics

Cybercriminals are well aware that remote workers are attractive targets due to the combination of technical vulnerabilities in home-office setups and the potential for exploiting human weaknesses. Unlike their colleagues in the office, people working remotely face the challenge of not being able to easily approach someone in person to inquire about a specific request mentioned in a chat message or email. Remote workers often have more flexibility in their work schedules, allowing them to deviate from normal business hours. However, remote workers often do not receive the same level of benefits as their in-office counterparts when it comes to utilizing advanced technology suites that safeguard against phishing and other social engineering attacks. Many people believe that remote workers are more susceptible to social engineering by criminals compared to those working in professional offices, due to various reasons. Remote workers have a higher tendency to fall victim to problematic emails, dangerous links, or unintentionally comply with requests from criminals.." Remote workers need to remain highly cautious of social engineering attacks.

Exploring Cybersecurity Insurance

If you think that your business could face a devastating loss or even collapse due to a breach, purchasing cybersecurity insurance might be worth considering, even though it may seem excessive for most small businesses. It's important to note that most cybersecurity insurance policies have carve-outs or exclusions. Therefore, it's crucial to have a clear understanding of what is covered, what is not, and the extent of your coverage for potential damages. If your business experiences a breach and fails as a result, relying on a policy that only covers two hours of data restoration by an expert will not provide much value. Insurers typically need businesses to meet a specific cybersecurity standard to purchase and maintain coverage. In certain situations, the insurance company may deny a claim if it determines that the insured party's negligence or failure to comply with policy requirements contributed to the breach.

Ensuring the security of employee data

You have to safeguard confidential data about your employees. Failure to adequately safeguard this information may result in negative consequences with government regulators, your employees, or the public. This is a good practice for securing physical files. It is recommended to use double-locking, which involves storing the paper files in a locked cabinet within a locked room. It is important to use different keys for each lock to enhance security. The electronic files should be securely stored within an encrypted and password-protected folder, drive, or virtual drive. Standards like these may not always be sufficient for every situation, so it's important to consult with an attorney for guidance. It is important to note the potential consequences of failing to protect employee information. In the event of a breach, where a criminal gains access to private employee data, you may face legal action from affected employees and former employees. Additionally, the government may impose fines on your business. The costs of remediation can often exceed the expenses that would have been incurred through proactive prevention. Additionally, the negative consequences of bad publicity on a business's sales can be devastating, potentially leading to its downfall. It's important to keep in mind that certain types of information, such as employee personnel records, W2 forms, Social Security numbers, I9 employment eligibility forms, home addresses, and phone numbers, medical information including COVID-19 test results and/or vaccination records, and any other health-related information that you may have, as well as vacation records and family leave records, are considered private. It is always better to be cautious and treat any uncertain information as private.

PCI DSS

The Payment Card Industry Data Security Standard (PCI DSS) is a crucial information security standard that applies to organizations responsible for handling major credit cards and the associated data. The standard has undergone several updates and expansions over time. The latest version, Version 3.2.1, was published in May 2018. Although all companies, regardless of their size, are required to comply with the PCI DSS standard, it does consider the varying levels of resources that different businesses have at their disposal. There are four distinct levels of PCI Compliance. The level of compliance required by an organization is typically determined by the volume of credit card transactions it handles annually. Additionally, other factors, such as the level of risk associated with the payments received by the company, are taken into consideration.

Here are the different levels:

- **PCI Level 4:** Standards for businesses processing fewer than 20,000 credit card transactions per year.
- **PCI Level 3** is designed for businesses that handle a moderate volume of credit card transactions, ranging from 20,000 to 1,000,000 per year.
- **PCI Level 2** applies to businesses that handle a moderate volume of credit card transactions, ranging from 1,000,000 to 6,000,000 per year.
- **PCI Level 1:** Standards for businesses that handle over 6,000,000 credit card transactions annually

Extensive literature exists on the topic, with numerous organizations providing specialized classes. If you run a small business and handle credit card transactions or store credit card information for any other purpose, it is important to seek the assistance of a knowledgeable professional in PCI compliance. Your credit card processors often have the expertise to suggest a suitable consultant or assist you directly.

Laws regarding the disclosure of breaches

Recently, several jurisdictions have implemented breach disclosure laws that oblige businesses to publicly disclose any suspicions of a breach that may have put certain types of stored information at risk. The laws regarding breach disclosure can differ significantly depending on the jurisdiction. Surprisingly, even small businesses may be subject to these laws in certain cases. It is important to have a good understanding of the laws that pertain to your business. In the unfortunate event of a breach, the government should not penalize you for any mishandling of the situation. Keep in mind that a significant number of small businesses do not survive after experiencing a breach. The involvement of the government in such situations can further decrease the chances of your business's survival following a successful cyberattack. The laws that pertain to your business may encompass not only those of the jurisdiction where you are physically situated but also the jurisdictions of the individuals for whom you are managing information.

GDPR

The General Data Protection Regulation (GDPR) is a European privacy regulation that came into effect in 2018. It applies to all businesses that handle consumer data of residents in the European Union, regardless of their size, industry, or country of origin. It also applies regardless of whether the EU resident is physically located within the EU. There are strict penalties imposed on businesses that fail to adequately safeguard the personal data of EU residents. This regulation highlights the potential impact on small businesses in New York that sell items to EU residents. It emphasizes the importance of complying with GDPR to protect the personal data of purchasers and avoid potential penalties. In July 2019, the United Kingdom's Information Commissioner's Office (ICO) announced fines for British Airways and Marriott. British Airways was fined approximately $230 million, while Marriott faced a fine of around $123 million. These fines were imposed due to GDPR-related violations that occurred as a result of data breaches. The GDPR can be quite intricate. If you believe that your business could potentially fall under the scope of GDPR, it would be advisable to consult with a lawyer who specializes in this area of law.

There is no need to worry about GDPR. Although small businesses in the United States may technically fall under the jurisdiction of GDPR, it is highly unlikely that the EU will prioritize penalizing these businesses that do not operate in Europe shortly. The EU has more pressing matters to address. However, it is important not to overlook GDPR as American small businesses could potentially face enforcement actions in the future.

HIPAA

The privacy of individuals' medical information is a top priority under federal law in the United States. Parties responsible for housing healthcare-related data must ensure its protection. The

Health Insurance Portability and Accountability Act (HIPAA), which was implemented in 1996, impose severe penalties for the mishandling of such information. It is important to determine if HIPAA applies to your business and, if so, make sure that you are effectively safeguarding the relevant data following industry standards or higher. Numerous jurisdictions worldwide have regulations that bear resemblance to HIPAA.

Biometric data

If you use any forms of biometric authentication or store biometric data for any reason, you may be required to comply with privacy and security laws that govern such data. Several states have already passed laws on this matter, and it is expected that more will do the same.

Laws regarding the prevention of money laundering

The purpose of anti-money laundering laws is to hinder criminals from transforming illegally acquired funds into funds that appear to be obtained through legal means. It is important for individuals using cryptocurrency to be aware of and comply with anti-money laundering laws, even if they are not financial institutions. This ensures that their transactions with unknown parties are conducted within legal boundaries.

Global restrictions

This can be a legal concern when paying ransomware ransoms, particularly if the recipients of the payments are subject to sanctions, as conducting any financial transactions with them would be a federal crime. Although individuals who have paid ransoms have not faced prosecution by the U.S. government for breaking these laws, there are signs that the leniency towards these violations may be diminishing.

Managing Internet Access

Small businesses encounter unique obstacles when it comes to Internet access and information systems, requiring them to be proactive in safeguarding against potential risks.

Separate Internet access for personal devices

It is advisable to set up a separate network for Internet access in your place of business. This will ensure that the network used for running your business remains unaffected and secure. Many modern routers provide this feature, typically labeled as a Guest network, within their configuration settings.

Implement policies for employees to bring their own devices (BYOD)

Establish clear policies and implement appropriate technology to safeguard your data when employees use their personal laptops or mobile devices for business purposes. Do not depend solely on policies. Failure to implement proper policies and technology safeguards may result in the devastating loss of data in the event of an employee's misconduct or error. Typically, small businesses shouldn't implement a bring-your-own-device (BYOD) policy, despite any potential allure it may have. In most cases, small businesses often neglect to properly protect data when employees use their own devices for work-related activities. This can lead to problems if an employee leaves the organization, especially if the departure is less than ideal. Android keyboards can gather information about a user's activities while they type. Although this type of learning can enhance spelling correction and word prediction, it also raises concerns about personal devices retaining sensitive corporate information as suggested content, even after an employee has left the employer.

It is important to establish clear policies and procedures for allowing BYOD, including guidelines for usage and decommissioning company technology on these devices. Additionally, it is crucial to have protocols in place for removing company data when an employee departs. Create a comprehensive mobile device security plan that encompasses remote wipe capabilities, strict enforcement of password protection and safeguarding of sensitive data, isolation of work-related data in a secure area of the device (referred to as sandboxing), installation, operation, and regular updates of mobile-optimized security software, strict prohibition of staff from utilizing public Wi-Fi for sensitive work-related activities, implementation of restrictions on certain activities while corporate data is present on the devices and more.

Ensure efficient management of inbound access

The Internet presents a notable distinction between individuals and businesses when it comes to the requirement of businesses to grant inbound access to untrusted parties. External parties need to have the capability to initiate communications that establish connections with the internal servers of your business. As an illustration, if a business wants to sell products online, it needs to grant access to its website for untrusted parties to make purchases. Parties accessing the website need to establish connections with payment systems and internal order tracking systems, despite their lack of trustworthiness. (In general, individuals are not required to grant any form of inbound access to their computers.) There is a significant distinction between businesses and individuals when it comes to inbound access.

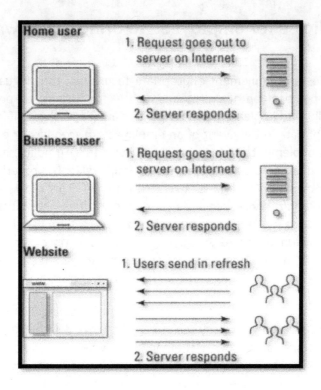

Although small businesses can secure web servers and email servers, the truth is that very few, if any, small businesses have the necessary resources to do so effectively, unless they specialize in cybersecurity. Small businesses should consider using third-party software and infrastructure, which can be set up and managed by experts, to host any systems used for inbound access.

There are several approaches that a business can consider:

- Use a well-known retailer's website. The websites of major retailers, like Amazon, Rakuten, and/or eBay, act as a significant barrier between your business's systems and the outside world if you exclusively sell items through them. The security teams at those companies protect their customer-facing systems from potential attacks. This system is often designed in a way that small businesses don't need to deal with incoming communications. And if they do, the communications come from the retailers' systems, not from the general public. There are various factors to consider when deciding whether to sell through a major retailer. It's worth noting that online markets often charge significant commissions. Consider the security advantages when evaluating the factors in making such a decision.
- Consider using a retail platform hosted by a third-party. In this scenario, the third party takes care of the majority of the infrastructure and security aspects, while you have the freedom to customize and manage your online store. This model may not provide the same level of isolation from outside users as the previous one, but it does offer

129

significantly better protection against attacks compared to running your platform. Shopify is a widely used third-party platform.

- Use a platform operated by a third party, which is also accountable for security measures. This approach provides enhanced protection compared to self-managed security, although it does not completely isolate your code from potential external threats seeking vulnerabilities and attempting attacks. It also requires you to take responsibility for the maintenance and security of the platform.
- You have the option to operate your system, whether it's hosted internally or externally, and enlist the help of a managed services provider to handle your security. It is important to note that you bear full responsibility for the security of the platform and infrastructure while entrusting a third party with the majority of the necessary tasks to fulfill that responsibility.

Defend your system from denial-of-service attacks

It is crucial to have security technology in place to safeguard your Internet-facing sites from potential denial-of-service (DoS) attacks. It's highly probable that retailers already have it if you're selling through them. If you're utilizing a third-party cloud platform, the provider may also offer it. If you're managing the site independently, it's crucial to secure protection to prevent any potential disruptions that could harm your site and business. Several companies specialize in offering this kind of protection.

Consider using HTTPS

For businesses with websites, it is crucial to have a valid TLS/SSL certificate installed. This ensures that users can securely communicate with the site and have confidence that it is owned by your business. Security systems that guard against DoS attacks often include a certificate as part of their package.

VPN

The VPN should establish a secure tunnel between your remote users and your business, rather than between users and a VPN provider when it comes to remote access. The tunnel provides a secure connection for remote users, safeguarding their communications and granting them access to exclusive business resources as if they were physically present in the company's offices.

Conduct penetration tests

Many individuals and small businesses often neglect to conduct tests to determine the vulnerability of their systems to hackers. Undertaking this task can prove to be quite valuable, particularly when implementing a new system or upgrading network infrastructure.

Exercise caution when using IoT devices

Connected cameras, alarms, and other security measures are commonly used by businesses nowadays. It is crucial to assign someone to oversee the security of these devices. Additionally, it is recommended to run them on separate networks or virtual segments from any computers used for business operations. Ensure strict control over device access and prohibit employees from connecting any unauthorized IoT devices to the company's networks. It is advisable to only purchase IoT devices from reputable manufacturers. For instance, it is not advisable to solely focus on purchasing the cheapest connected cameras available online, without considering the manufacturer or the origin of the product.

Use multiple network segments

Considering the size and nature of your business, it might be a prudent decision to separate different computers onto distinct network segments. A software development company needs to have separate networks for developers and operations personnel. This ensures that the coding process is not hindered by activities related to payroll and accounts payable. The same applies to remote home-based workers. It is important to keep personal and work networks separate.

Exercise caution when using payment cards

You need to have a conversation with your processor regarding the different anti-fraud technology options that may be available to you if you accept credit and/or debit cards and are not selling through a major retailer's website.

Addressing Power Problems

It is highly recommended to use an uninterruptible power supply (UPS) for systems that must remain operational without any interruptions. Ensure that UPSs are not overloaded by verifying their capacity to handle the combined load of all connected devices. Additionally, it is important to ensure that the power supplies can sustain the systems for a duration longer than any anticipated power interruption. If you sell a range of products and services through online retail, the impact of your ability to sell going offline, even for a brief period, can be detrimental. It can result in lost sales, both immediate and potential, and can also harm your reputation.

Frequently Asked Questions

1. How do you think businesses and organizations should keep off cyber criminals?
2. What do you understand by cybersecurity insurance?
3. How do you manage internet access in cybersecurity?

CHAPTER ELEVEN
PURSUING A CYBERSECURITY CAREER

Overview

In chapter eleven, you will get to see the multiple and different cyber security career opportunities you can explore and make money from.

Cybersecurity Career

In today's world, the demand for skilled cybersecurity professionals is higher than ever before. This presents a unique opportunity for individuals looking to embark on a career in cybersecurity, as the demand continues to increase over time. This surge can be attributed to the rise in high-profile ransomware attacks that have had a direct impact on people's quality of life. Additionally, the COVID-19 pandemic has led to a sudden and substantial increase in remote working, further fueling the need for cybersecurity expertise. This trend is expected to persist in the future. There is a significant shortage of qualified cybersecurity professionals to meet the increasing demand for these roles. The number of job openings in cybersecurity is growing at a faster rate than the available talent pool. Due to the scarcity of cybersecurity professionals about the demand for their skills, compensation packages for these individuals have consistently ranked among the highest in the technology industry.

Roles in Cybersecurity

Cybersecurity professionals have diverse responsibilities that depend on their specific roles. Their main objective is to safeguard data and systems from compromise. In certain government positions, their task may involve breaching systems and compromising adversary data. There is no singular career path known as "**cybersecurity**." The profession is filled with various nuances and offers different paths for career progression. It's worth mentioning that the job titles for roles in the field of information security, especially cybersecurity, often use the term "**security**" instead of explicitly stating "**cybersecurity**," "information security," or "**IT security**."

Experienced in the field of security engineering

There are various types of security engineers, with the majority being highly skilled technical professionals who specialize in constructing, managing, and troubleshooting information security systems for different types of organizations, such as corporate, government, or nonprofit projects. Security engineers in the professional services arms of vendors play a crucial role in ensuring the secure deployment of software at client sites.

Security manager

Security managers are usually found in mid-level management positions within larger enterprises. They are tasked with overseeing a specific area of information security. There may be one security manager who is in charge of handling all of a firm's security training, while another is responsible for overseeing the Internet-facing firewalls. Security managers usually focus more on overseeing and coordinating security efforts rather than directly engaging in technical security tasks, which are typically handled by their subordinates.

Security director

Security directors are responsible for overseeing information security within an organization. In smaller firms, the director typically assumes the role of the chief information security officer (CISO). In larger firms, there are often multiple directors who oversee different aspects of the information security program. These individuals typically report to the CISO.

Chief information security officer (CISO)

The CISO holds the crucial role of ensuring information security across an organization. The CISO role can be likened to the chief of staff of the organization's information-security defensive military. The CISO holds a high-ranking position in the management hierarchy. Being a CISO typically demands a strong background in management and extensive experience, along with a deep understanding of information security.

Security analyst

Security analysts are dedicated to proactively preventing information security breaches. The team thoroughly examines both current systems and upcoming threats, including new vulnerabilities, to maintain the organization's security.

Security architect

Security architects are responsible for designing and overseeing the implementation of information security countermeasures within organizations. This role requires a deep understanding of complex security infrastructures. Security professionals are often involved in projects outside of their department, such as assisting in the design of security measures for custom applications or providing guidance to networking teams in the design of corporate IT networking infrastructure.

Security administrator

Security administrators are skilled professionals who are responsible for the implementation, configuration, operation, management, and troubleshooting of information security countermeasures for an organization. These individuals are often the go-to experts for nontechnical professionals who encounter issues and require assistance from a security specialist.

Security auditor

Security auditors are responsible for conducting thorough security audits. Their main objective is to ensure that all security policies, procedures, and technologies are functioning as intended. By doing so, they can effectively protect corporate data, systems, and networks.

Cryptographer

Cryptographers are highly skilled professionals who specialize in the field of encryption, which is crucial for safeguarding sensitive information. Cryptographers focus on creating encryption systems to safeguard sensitive data, while cryptanalysts take on the task of analyzing encrypted information and encryption systems to decrypt the data. Cryptographers tend to be more prevalent in government agencies, the military, and academia, compared to other information security jobs. For government jobs in cryptography in the United States, U.S. citizenship and an active security clearance are necessary.

Vulnerability assessment analyst

Analysts specializing in vulnerability assessment meticulously scrutinize computer systems, databases, networks, and other components of the information infrastructure to identify any potential vulnerabilities. Explicit permission is required for individuals working in such positions. While penetration testers are discussed in the following section, vulnerability assessors take on a different role. They operate as insiders with access to systems, allowing them to thoroughly examine them from the beginning.

Ethical hacker

The work of ethical hackers involves deliberately targeting systems and networks with the explicit permission of their owners. Their goal is to identify security vulnerabilities that can be addressed and resolved. Penetration testers or pen-testers are often referred to as ethical hackers. Many corporations have their ethical hackers, but many professionals in this field work for consulting companies and provide their services to third parties.

Security researcher

Security researchers are individuals who have a keen eye for identifying vulnerabilities in current systems and assessing the potential security risks associated with emerging technologies and products. They occasionally devise fresh security models and approaches through their research. From an ethical standpoint and following the law in many jurisdictions, hacking an organization without explicit permission is considered illegal and does not align with the principles of being a security researcher or an ethical hacker.

Offensive hacker

Malicious hackers make deliberate attempts to infiltrate the systems of their adversaries to cause damage or steal valuable information. It is against the law for a business in the United States of America to engage in offensive actions, such as retaliating against hackers attempting to breach their systems. All legal offensive hacking jobs in the United States are in government positions, specifically within intelligence agencies and the armed forces. If you have a passion for offensive security and are looking for opportunities beyond ethical hacking, you might consider exploring a career in the government or military. Security clearances are often a requirement for many offensive hacking positions.

Software security engineer

Security is seamlessly integrated into software during the design and development process by software security engineers. The software is thoroughly tested to ensure it is free from any vulnerability. They might even be the ones who wrote the software.

Software source code security auditor

The source code of programs is thoroughly reviewed by software source code security auditors. Their goal is to identify programming errors, vulnerabilities, violations of corporate policies and standards, regulatory problems, copyright infringement, and other issues that require attention. Resolving these issues is crucial for ensuring the security and integrity of the software.

Security consultant

There is a wide variety of security consultants available. Many individuals, such as myself, offer guidance to corporate executives regarding security strategy, provide expert testimony, or contribute to the growth and success of security companies. Some individuals prefer a more hands-on approach to penetration testing. Some individuals may specialize in designing or operating specific technologies within a security infrastructure. Positions in the field of information security can be found in a wide range of areas when it comes to security consulting.

Security expert witness

Security expert witnesses are individuals who possess extensive experience in the specific field of security in which they are called upon to provide testimony. These experts are entrusted by judges to offer their knowledgeable opinions on matters that are under litigation.

Security specialist

Various roles fall under the title of security specialist. Experience in the information security field is typically a prerequisite for the various roles.

Member of the incident response team

The incident response team is composed of the primary individuals responsible for addressing security incidents. The team members strive to effectively manage and mitigate attacks, aiming to minimize the resulting damage. They frequently analyze to determine the cause of events, occasionally finding that no corrective action is necessary. Incident responders can be compared to cybersecurity firefighters. They handle dangerous attacks and are occasionally called upon to confirm the absence of a fire.

Expert in forensic analysis

The work of forensic analysts involves investigating computer events, examining data, computers, computing devices, and networks to gather evidence, analyze it, and preserve it accurately. Their goal is to determine the details of what occurred, how it occurred, and identify the responsible party. Forensic analysts can be compared to investigators from law enforcement and insurance companies who meticulously examine properties following a fire, aiming to uncover the cause and identify those accountable.

Cybersecurity regulations expert

Experts in cybersecurity regulations possess extensive knowledge of the various regulations about cybersecurity. Their role is to assist organizations in achieving compliance with these regulations. They typically have prior experience working with various compliance-type matters, although they are not always attorneys.

Privacy regulations expert

Experts in privacy regulations are well-versed in the various rules and regulations surrounding privacy. They play a crucial role in helping organizations maintain compliance with these regulations. They typically have previous experience dealing with a range of compliance-related issues, although not all of them are necessarily lawyers.

Exploring Different Career Paths

It is important for individuals to carefully consider their long-term goals when planning their careers. If you have aspirations of becoming a CISO, it would be beneficial to gain experience in various practical roles, obtain an MBA, and strive for promotions and certifications in the field of information security management. On the other hand, if your goal is to become a senior architect, it would be more advantageous to focus on progressing through different positions related to security analysis and design, engaging in penetration testing, and acquiring technical degrees. Here are some examples of potential career paths.

Career path: Senior security architect

Security architects in the United States often earn salaries exceeding $100,000, and in certain markets, even higher. This makes the position highly desirable for many individuals. **Although each individual's career trajectory is distinct, a common route to becoming a senior security architect may involve following a path similar to the one outlined below:**

1. **Do one of the following options:**
   - Obtain a bachelor's degree in computer science.
   - Obtain a degree in any field and complete an entry-level certification exam in cybersecurity, such as Security+.
   - Secure a technical position without a degree and showcase expertise in the relevant technologies used in the role.
2. Seeking a position as a network administrator or systems administrator to acquire valuable hands-on security experience.
3. Consider acquiring a more specialized credential, such as CEH, to enhance your expertise.
4. Experience as a security administrator is highly valued, particularly with a diverse range of security systems and a proven track record over an extended period.
5. Obtain one or more general security certifications, such as CISSP.
6. Consider pursuing a career as a security architect to gain valuable experience in this role.
7. Consider pursuing an advanced security architecture certification, such as CISSP-ISSAP.
8. Achieve the position of a senior-level security architect.

Becoming a senior-level architect doesn't happen overnight. It usually requires a decade or more of relevant experience to reach that position.

Career path: Chief Information Security Officer (CISO)

The salaries for chief information security officers in the United States are typically around $150,000 or higher, especially in certain industries. However, these positions can be quite demanding and stressful, which may be why many CISOs choose to leave after only a few years. CISOs are responsible for ensuring corporate information security, which often means handling emergencies and receiving little recognition for success, but facing significant criticism when things go wrong. **Although each individual's career trajectory is distinct, a common route to becoming a CISO may involve following a path similar to the one outlined below:**

1. Obtain a bachelor's degree in computer science or information technology.
2. **Do one of the following options:**
   - Seek employment in a hands-on technical role such as systems analyst, systems engineer, programmer, or a similar position.
   - Work as a network engineer.

3. Explore opportunities in the field of security and consider roles such as security engineer, security analyst, or security consultant. By taking on different positions within an

organization or working as a consultant, you can gain exposure to various aspects of information security.

4. Consider obtaining general certifications in information security, such as CISSP.
5. Transition into a leadership role by managing a team responsible for security operations. It would be ideal to gradually oversee multiple information security teams, each specializing in different areas of information security.
6. **Carry out one of the following options:**
- Pursue a master's degree in cybersecurity, preferably with a specialization in information security management.
- Pursue a master's degree in computer science, preferably with a specialization in cybersecurity.
- Pursue a master's degree in information systems management, preferably with a specialization in information security.
- Pursue an MBA.
7. **Do one of the below options:**
- Aim to become a divisional CISO (either de facto or de jure).
- Take on the role of CISO in a smaller business or nonprofit organization.
8. Acquire an advanced information security credential that specializes in information security management, such as CISSP-ISSMP.
9. Take on the role of Chief Information Security Officer (CISO) in a larger organization.

Becoming a CISO can be a lengthy journey, often spanning several years or even decades, particularly in larger organizations.

Getting Started in Information Security

It is common for individuals in the field of information security to have started their careers in other areas of information technology. Some individuals were introduced to the fascinating realm of cybersecurity during their time in technical roles. In different scenarios, individuals pursued technical roles that were not directly related to information security. However, they intended to enhance their skill set and leverage these positions as a pathway into the field of security. Positions in risk analysis, systems engineering and development, and networking can serve as excellent starting points for your career. A knowledgeable email administrator, for instance, will gain extensive knowledge of email security as well as secure network designs and server security. Individuals involved in the development of web-based systems often acquire knowledge of web security and secure software design. System and network administrators will gain valuable insights into the security of the items under their care, ensuring their continued functionality and well-being.

Here are some technical jobs that can help prepare you for cybersecurity-related roles:

- Programmer (also referred to as a coder)
- Software engineer
- Web developer

- Information systems support engineer (technical support hands-on specialist)
- Systems administrator
- Email Administrator
- Network administrator
- Database administrator
- Website administrator

Certain positions outside of the technical field can also provide valuable preparation for careers in non-technical roles within information security.

Here are a few examples:

- Auditor
- Detective in law enforcement
- Lawyer specializing in legal aspects of cybersecurity
- An attorney specializing in regulatory compliance
- An attorney specializing in privacy-related areas of law
- Analyst specializing in risk management

Exploring Popular Certifications

Cybersecurity certifications and certificates demonstrating completion of cybersecurity courses can demonstrate to employers that you possess the necessary knowledge and skills in this field, aiding your career progression. There is a wide range of information-security certifications available in the market today. Some specialize in certain technologies or aspects of information security, while others have a broader scope. It is important to note that certifying bodies constantly update their certification requirements and curricula to stay abreast of the ever-evolving field of cybersecurity. Therefore, it is advisable to acquire an up-to-date study guide when preparing for a certification exam.

CISSP

The CISSP certification, which was first introduced in 1994, encompasses a wide range of security-related domains, with varying levels of depth in different areas. This text highlights the importance of workers having a comprehensive understanding of various aspects of information security. It emphasizes that broad knowledge is valuable and necessary for those in higher positions in information security management. Employers can find comfort in knowing that their workers possess this broad knowledge. The CISSP is typically pursued by individuals who have gained significant experience in the information security field. Although it is possible to take the CISSP exam without prior experience, the credential is only awarded after fulfilling the necessary years of work in the field. Due to their extensive experience and CISSP credentials, individuals in this field often earn higher salaries compared to their uncertified peers and counterparts with different certifications. The CISSP credential, issued by the (ISC)2 organization, is known for its high regard and vendor neutrality. It is also considered more evergreen compared to other certifications. The CISSP exam offers a wide range of study materials and training courses.

Additionally, it provides the convenience of being administered in numerous locations and on various dates, making it more accessible compared to other cybersecurity certifications. There are additional options for those who want to demonstrate their expertise in information security architecture (CISSP-ISSAP), management (CISSP-ISSMP), and engineering (CISSP-ISSEP). The CISSP credentials from (ISC)2 come with a specific Code of Ethics that holders must adhere to. Additionally, individuals are required to engage in ongoing education activities to keep their credentials up to date. These credentials need to be renewed every three years. The CISSP does not aim to assess practical technical abilities, and it does not do so. If individuals are seeking to showcase their expertise in particular technologies or areas of technology, such as penetration testing, security administration, auditing, and more, they may find it beneficial to pursue either a specialized certification that focuses on technical skills or certifications that are specific to certain products and skills.

CISM

The Certified Information Security Manager (CISM) credential from the Information Systems Audit and Control Association (ISACA) has gained significant popularity since its introduction approximately two decades ago. Coming from an organization with a strong emphasis on audit and controls, the CISM credential tends to have a narrower focus compared to the CISSP. It delves into policies, procedures, and technologies for managing and controlling information security systems, particularly within larger enterprises or organizations. Similar to the CISSP, obtaining a CISM certification requires candidates to possess a significant amount of professional experience in the field of information security. The CISSP and CISM have distinct focuses, with the former emphasizing technical subjects and the latter concentrating on management-related topics. However, there is also a significant overlap between the two offerings. Both have earned a great deal of respect.

CEH

The Certified Ethical Hacker (CEH), provided by the International Council of E-Commerce Consultants (EC-Council), is designed for individuals with a minimum of two years of professional experience who are committed to establishing their reputation as ethical hackers, also known as penetration testers. The CEH exam assesses candidates' abilities in various aspects of hacking, including reconnaissance, network penetration, privilege escalation, and data theft. This exam covers a range of practical skills, including attack vehicles like different types of malware, attack techniques such as SQL injection, cryptanalysis methods used to undermine encryption, methods of social engineering to exploit human error in technical defenses, and strategies for evading detection by covering tracks. The maintenance of a CEH credential is crucial for individuals who hold the EC-Council's CEH certification. This requirement emphasizes the importance of staying up-to-date with the ever-evolving technologies in today's fast-paced world.

Security+

Security+ is a certification that holds great value, particularly for individuals who are just starting in their careers. It is a vendor-neutral certification that covers a wide range of cybersecurity topics. It is provided and managed by CompTIA, a highly regarded nonprofit organization focused on technology education. Although there is no specific requirement for a minimum number of years of professional experience to obtain a CompTIA Security+ designation, it is generally recommended to have some practical experience in the field before attempting the exam. This experience can greatly increase the chances of passing the exam successfully. The Security+ exam provides a comprehensive understanding of technical concepts, making it ideal for individuals pursuing roles in entry-level IT auditing, penetration testing, systems administration, network administration, and security administration. As a result, CompTIA Security+ serves as a valuable certification for those starting their careers in the field. Continuing education credits are required for individuals who have earned the Security+ designation since 2011 to maintain their credentials.

GSEC

The GSEC is an entry-level security certification that covers materials in courses offered by the SANS Institute, a highly regarded information-security training company. The GSEC certification offers a significant amount of practical, hands-on material, distinguishing it from the CISM or CISSP certifications. This makes it more valuable in certain situations and less desirable in others. The GSEC exam is often considered more challenging and comprehensive compared to the Security+ designation, despite being marketed as entry-level. All GSEC credential holders must demonstrate ongoing professional experience or educational advancement in the realm of information security to uphold their credentials.

Verifiability

Employers can easily verify if a person holds the credentials they claim, thanks to the issuers of major information security credentials. Verification for security purposes may involve the user's certification identification number, which is generally not made public by credential holders. It is important to regularly update your information in the issuer's database if you have obtained a certification. It is crucial to ensure that you do not risk losing your certification due to a lack of reminders for submitting continuing education credits or paying maintenance fees.

Ethics

This code of ethics for security certifications emphasizes the importance of not only following laws and regulations but also behaving in a manner that goes beyond mere compliance. It is important to fully comprehend these requirements. When someone loses a credential because of unethical behavior, it can have a detrimental impact on the trust others have in them and can lead to various negative consequences for their information security career.

Overcoming a Criminal Record

Although a criminal record does not necessarily hinder someone from securing numerous cybersecurity-related jobs, it can pose a significant obstacle in obtaining specific positions. If any factors would prevent someone from obtaining a security clearance, it would disqualify them from certain government and government-contractor roles. Employers often take into consideration the nature, timing, and age at which one committed past crimes when making hiring decisions. Certain information-security organizations may be open to hiring a reformed, former teenage hacker, but may have reservations about hiring someone with a conviction for a violent crime as an adult. Similarly, individuals who have completed their sentences for computer crimes committed many years ago and have maintained a clean record since then may be perceived differently by prospective employers compared to those who were recently released from prison for similar offenses.

Conquering Bad Credit

For those who are not well-versed in the security industry, the importance of a credit score might not be immediately apparent when considering potential employers. However, there are instances where it does come into play. This is because credit reports are reviewed as part of the background check process for government positions requiring clearance. Clearances can be denied if reviewers have concerns about the applicant's reliability or the potential for them to be tempted to sell information due to financial problems. If you are applying for a position that requires a clearance and you have a less-than-ideal credit score due to circumstances beyond your control, it might be a good idea to address this matter with the relevant parties in advance.

Exploring Alternative Careers with a Focus on Cybersecurity

There are numerous opportunities to work in fields that closely interact with cybersecurity professionals and benefit from the growing global focus on cybersecurity. Legal professionals have the option to focus their practice on areas such as cybersecurity laws or ensuring companies adhere to privacy regulations. Similarly, law enforcement officials can gain expertise in the field of cybercrime investigation and forensic techniques. Cybersecurity has undoubtedly generated, is generating, and will continue to generate numerous profitable professional prospects across various industries. Anyone can benefit from the discipline's boom, regardless of technical expertise. If you have a keen interest in cybersecurity, there are numerous rewarding opportunities for you to explore.

Frequently Asked Questions

1. What are the job roles in cybersecurity?
2. What do you understand by information security?
3. What are the different popular certifications in cybersecurity?

4. How do you explore alternative careers in cybersecurity?
5. How do you overcome a criminal record?

CONCLUSION

It has become increasingly common for people to be online, but it is important to take certain precautions to ensure their safety. Cybersecurity refers to the measures implemented to safeguard computer systems from unauthorized access or attack. The primary goal of cybersecurity is to protect the well-being, assets, and reputation of individuals. It's crucial to exercise caution when exploring unfamiliar websites and downloading content onto your devices. It is important to thoroughly review the privacy policies of websites and seek guidance from parents or other trusted adults. Here are some guidelines to ensure your online safety.

Ensure that your personal information remains confidential. You should also refrain from sharing personal information online. It is important to refrain from disclosing personal information such as your name, school name, parent name, address, phone number, social security number, birthdate, passwords, and other sensitive details. Be aware that this information could potentially grant cyber criminals access to your location, home, or school. Exercise caution when sharing personal information online, especially on websites that are not trustworthy. All websites need to begin with https:// to ensure trust and security. If you're having trouble seeing it, keep an eye out for a closed padlock symbol located on the left or right side of the web address (URL). When you click on the padlock, a message will appear showing the company name and a notification stating that the connection to the server is encrypted. On the other hand, if the lock is open, it means that the website is untrusted. It's important to be cautious of counterfeit versions of websites you frequently visit.

As an illustration, it is important to look for logos that have a lighter color and to verify that the link includes the accurate domain name (e.g., www.disney.com or www.facebook.com). Always double-check the URL of every website you visit to ensure you're on the correct site. Beware of fraudulent websites that can compromise your personal information and share it with cybercriminals. Be cautious of counterfeit sites that may include additional characters in the URL, such as www.disney1.com. No need for the 1. Additionally, creating strong passwords is a common requirement for most websites. They often ask for a combination of numbers, letters, and symbols to enhance security. It is recommended to use a mix of uppercase and lowercase letters, numbers, symbols, and a minimum of eight characters when creating passwords. It is important to avoid using easily guessable passwords such as your name, pet's name, or date of birth. Instead, consider combining these with a complex mix of numbers, letters, and symbols. It is important to use a combination of letters and numbers, rather than using only letters or only numbers.

If you struggle to remember all of your passwords, consider using a password manager. It is important to avoid saving passwords in your web browser unless you have anti-virus software installed. Consider carefully before sharing anything on the internet. Information that is posted

143

online remains accessible indefinitely. Ensure you maintain a positive online presence on your social media pages. A post has the potential to reach a vast audience, spanning thousands or even millions of people. Avoid discussing or sharing content about individuals. Please refrain from sharing explicit images of yourself or others. It is important to refrain from sharing personal information, whether it is about yourself or others.

INDEX

E

F

I

J

Modern-day governments, 47

modifying the default IP address, 56

monitor and control both incoming and outgoing network traffic, 13

more advanced sites, 49

more deceptive variations of cybercrime, 1

more difficult to maintain privacy, 60

more elusive, 43

most computers are not regularly updated, 35

most cybersecurity insurance policies, 124

Most opportunistic attacks are driven by the desire for financial gain, 35

most prevalent method of compromising, 34

mother's maiden name, 6, 34, 61

mother's maiden name by looking, 61

Motivate your staff, 116

motivations behind launching DDoS attacks, 24

multiple areas of cybersecurity and beyond, 70

Multiple methods can be employed to gain access to a computing device., 17

multiple nodes before reaching their destination, 54

multiple parties, 38, 117

Multiprotocol Heterogeneous Network Environment, 112

multitude of security challenges, 1

my flight in ten minutes, 24

N

national security, 1, 12, 28

nation-states, 9, 10, 11, 31

Natural disasters, 46

Nature is not the sole contributor to the external problems, 46

NBT, 112

NBT Packets, 112

nearly every aspect of our lives is electronically tracked, 3

necessary permissions, 59

necessitate meticulous configuration and management., 75

negative image of a black hat, 40

NetBEUI, 112

Network administrator, 139

network and multiple users, 115

Network and Security Concepts, 5

network bandwidth, 8

network flooding, 8

Network Infrastructure Poisoning, 32

network of a cellular provider, 54

Network sniffing, 34

Networking equipment, 53

Networking equipment is vulnerable to hacking, 53

networks and devices, 43

networks and firewalls, 16

Newly discovered malware, 31

NIAG, 5, 6, 7, 8

NIST, 14

NMAP, 113

nonprofits, 27

non-public meetings, 123

Nonrepudiation, 6

Non-repudiation, 78

non-repudiation are tools that system designers, 5, 9

non-repudiation remains crucial and indispensable, 6

non-technical method utilized by attackers, 7

Not All Dangers Come From Attackers, 44

notorious cases like the ILOVEYOU worm, 10

Novices in the field of hacking, 40

now scanning social media, 49

numbers, symbols, and a minimum of eight characters, 143

numerous cybersecurity challenges, 93

Numerous industries, 68

numerous opportunities to work in fields that closely interact with cybersecurity professionals, 142

numerous security violations occurred, 98

numerous users experienced difficulties accessing multiple well-known websites, 23

O

objectives beyond financial gain,, 36

obstacles and intricacies, 13

Obtain a bachelor's degree in computer science or information technology., 137

Obtain a bachelor's degree in computer science., 137

obtain a CompTIA Security+ designation, 141

Obtain a degree in any field and complete an entry-level certification, 137

obtain an MBA, 136

obtained computing power and network bandwidth, 19

obtaining credit card numbers, 36

Offensive hacker, 135

P

security professionals must have a comprehensive understanding of three fundamental concepts, 5
security requirements for a cellphone, 50
Security researcher, 134
Security researchers are individuals, 134
Security software, 52, 54, 56, 58
security software subscription is expiring, 32
Security specialist, 135
security team comprises individuals, 5
security teams, 81, 82, 90, 91, 129, 138
security teams can enhance their capacity to identify IOCs, 91
security teams carefully monitor network traffic, 81
security vulnerabilities, 29, 35, 104, 112, 113, 114, 134
Security with Zero Trust, 76
Security+, 137, 141
Seek employment in a hands-on technical role, 137
seek guidance from parents or other trusted adults, 143
Seeking a position as a network administrator, 137
Select a random Personal Identification Number, 64
Selling data to unscrupulous competitors, 28
selling stolen lists, 36
send an email or browse the web., 76
Sending deceptive emails, 45
Sending deceptive emails impersonating CEOs, 45
Senior security architect, 137
sense of panic would ensue, 16
Separate Internet access for personal devices, 127
separate network from your computers, 65
serial numbers, 43
server's feature, 37
Session hijacking, 38
setting you apart from others, 5
settlement agreements, 88
settlements reaching millions of dollars., 7
several jurisdictions, 126
Several online platforms offer the option, 107
several trends are significantly influencing the future, 75
severe consequences of its loss or compromise, 68
severely impact businesses, 4
share threat intelligence and exchange best practices., 2
Sharing excessive amounts of information, 61
sharing of information, 79, 91
Shopify is a widely used third-party platform., 130

shopping app from a specific company, 102
Shoulder surfing, 7, 96
significant DDoS attack targeting, 23
significant number of attacks, 17
significant over the years., 44
significant portion of the population in the Western World, 49
significant profitability, 17
significant security risk, 56
significant transformation, 4, 53
significantly enhance, 12, 88, 105
significantly enhance the overall defense against cyber-attacks, 12
significantly enhances the security of organizations, 74
significantly expanding attack landscape, 3
significantly jeopardize your cybersecurity, 45
signs of slowing down, 4
similar information, 25
Similar to web servers, 32
simple Google search of a candidate's name, 48
simplifying device setup, 66
simulation of human intelligence processes by machines, 15
single exploit, 31
site's lack of proper security measures, 32
skill sets in the security career fields, 5
sleeping patterns, 50
small business experiences, 19
small business owners, 3, 60
Small business owners must prioritize employee education, 115
Smart devices, 65
Smishing, 25
Smishing involves instances of phishing where attackers send their messages, 25
SMS messages, 63
social cohesion are at stake, 4
Social engineering, 34, 45
Social engineering attacks, 34
Social engineering attacks involve criminals deceiving individuals, 34
social engineering is when a criminal poses as a member, 34
social engineering tactics, 15, 29, 124
social media accounts, 42, 62, 117, 118
social media platforms, 34, 37, 121
Social media platforms, 49
social media provider, 101
social media security settings, 62

T

U

V

W